THIS FOR
author's exp

MW01178618

End of London during World War Two. Kitty is not a child from the Kindertransport, but a Jewish Londoner who is evacuated along with the rest of London's children to the safety of the British countryside. But after lodging in a series of foster homes, she decides that not even the imminent threat of Nazi bombs can keep her away from her Mum and Uncle Yudi in London. A new epilogue brings the story up to war's end and the historic victory celebration outside Buckingham Palace.

Praise for **I'm Not Going Back**

"Kitty recounts life in a country village under the thumb of a dour and cold taskmaster. She is a spirited, determined youngster whose mind is set upon returning to London . . . . She is a very strong and engaging character, even at her young age." — *Jewish Book World*

"The details are absorbing . . . Kitty gets completely inside her young personality" — *London Jewish Chronicle*

"Like a friend telling you about her experiences over coffee." — *Marcia Weiss Posner, Association of Jewish Libraries*

"At each stage in [her] full life, Ms Wintrob has displayed the same spunk and spirit she did as a 10-year-old girl forced to leave her Jewish working-class home with no indication where she was going or when she would be back." — *National Post* (*Toronto*)

To

chistopher.

Sincerely

Stephentree.

June 2016

I'm Not Going Back

Wartime Memoir
of a Child Evacuee **by Kitty Wintrob**

Now and Then Books
Toronto 2014

ISBN 978-09919009-3-0

I'M NOT GOING BACK: WARTIME MEMOIR OF A CHILD
EVACUEE, by Kitty Wintrob; second edition, with a new
epilogue. Copyright © 2014 by Kitty Wintrob and Now &
Then Books. All rights reserved. No part of this publication
may be reproduced in any form or by any means, electronic,
mechanical or otherwise, except for brief passages quoted in
the context of a critical review, without prior permission from
Now & Then Books.

Library and Archives Canada Cataloguing in Publication

Wintrob, Kitty, author
    I'm not going back : wartime memoir of a child evacuee
/ by Kitty Wintrob. -- Second edition.

 Originally published: Toronto : Now & Then Books,
©2009. "Second edition with a new epilogue".
ISBN 978-0-9919009-3-0 (pbk.)
    1. World War, 1939-1945--Children--England--
London--Juvenile fiction. I. Title.

PS8645.I58I56 2014   jC813'.6   C2014-904441-0

To my beloved son Phillip, z"l, whose constant refrain was: "Mum, this is about the way kids are. You have to get it published!"

1

Waiting

IT WAS A NICE DAY. It wasn't even raining.

We were all lined up in the street outside our school. A red brick wall with white cement between the bricks went around the school. And the white stood out so bright because it was a sunny day.

It made me think of my drawings of cats on the wall. I would draw a wall just like this one with lines where the bricks joined and then draw a sad and lonely cat with long whiskers, her tail resting on the wall, green eyes staring up at the moon. Today I felt like that lonely cat.

We were lined up in pairs. My partner was Sadie Davidovitch. We were wearing our brown uniforms. It was almost September, but instead of wearing our pretty cream summer uniforms as we did from May to July, today we were wearing our winter uniforms. They were brown tunics, with a brown blazer, and a brown velour hat to match. And we carried our overcoats. My blazer was edged in blue cord, and I hated it so much. Our school was divided into houses: Venice, which was my blue; Winchester, which was yellow; Rhodes, which was purple; and Athens, which was green. The house colour edged our hat band and pullover, too. I hated being in Venice, simply because the blue was such a dirty blue, and the brown was a dirty brown, and the two colours didn't go together. How I wished I was in Winchester, with Sheila Foster, in her brown and yellow, looking as pretty as ever.

But here I was with Sadie. She was in my House. She was my partner. And she was my friend. That's why we were standing together that day holding hands . . . all of us sad and silent, on this nice August day, in our winter uniforms.

Our school was on a narrow street off the High Street, and on the other side of the street were our Mums. So many Mums. They were told not to come that day, but of course they came.

Suddenly I heard a loud whisper: "Kitty, be careful! Look after yourself! And stay with Sadie!"

I looked up. I looked across the street. And there was my Mum with all the other Mums. And even with so many of them there I heard her.

Her dark crinkly hair was pulled right back. She was wearing her best coat, the one she only wore when she went to see my Aunties, on Saturdays. And a handkerchief was by her nose. She was trying to stop herself from crying. And I tried not to cry, too.

"Kitty, you'll be all right dear, don't worry," she whispered again. "Just be careful. Be careful. And stay friends with Sadie."

We looked at each other across that street. How we had prepared for that day! A few days before we had gone to get our gas masks, because the government was sure that the first day of the war the Germans would drop gas bombs, mustard or lewisite gas or whatever, and we would all be gassed just like in the First World War. Then, it happened in the trenches. But this time everybody said it would happen in London and other big cities. So we had to have a gas mask.

Getting the mask was such a business. We were sent a special card to tell us where to go for our mask. Some had to go to a police station, some to the local labour exchange, others to the post office, where a little room had been set aside. And the masks had to really fit—tight under the chin to make sure no gas could get inside. They really fussed over us children to make sure the mask fitted properly. When I looked in the mirror with mine on I thought I looked like a bulldog, a British bulldog.

Then when we had our gas mask, we had to get an identity card, which we were told to keep in the gas mask case. And finally we had to get the case. There were all kinds of cases, let me tell you, fancy ones and plain ones. The richer you were the nicer the case, the poorer the plainer. My case was the black ordinary kind, and we had to carry that gas mask in its case wherever we went.

For several days we had been going to school, even though it was August and we usually never started school until September. But a notice had come saying we would have to go to school earlier because any day we would be evacuated and we had to be prepared. Every day we took the one little suitcase we were allowed with us. Inside was a change of underwear, and two extra school blouses. That was all we were allowed: one change of underwear and one change of clothes.

Then, on Thursday, we were given the news: tomorrow we would be going away. No parents were to come to the school. No parents were to come to the station. And nobody knew where we would be going!

2

Embarking

SUDDENLY OUR HEADMISTRESS, Dr. Hunt, called all the teachers together and they went into a little huddle at the end of the street. Then Miss Harris, our form mistress, came over to us. She taught gym and always wore a gym tunic except, of course, today. To us she looked like a man, with very short cropped hair and a deep voice. But she always showed that she cared about us.

"All right girls," she said. "Everyone hold your partner's hand and we'll walk very quickly and very quietly to the station."

We turned and in our lines started up the road to the High Street. Our Mums were on the other side of the street. They were walking just as quickly and just as quietly in the same direction.

"Hurry up girls, hurry up, and don't look over the road," Miss Harris kept on saying. She sounded like a real Sergeant-Major.

I kept on looking over to my Mum, when Miss Harris wasn't looking, and waving. My Mum was waving all the time and holding her hankie up to her nose.

We passed so many familiar places. First there was Poppy's, a sweet shop just by the tram stop. This was where I got off to come to school. I had to come a long way as I had won a scholarship and this was the school I had chosen. We used to go into Poppy's and buy lovely toffee apples. The shop was so clean, with the glass jars of sweets lined along white-painted shelves, and the floor and counter all bright black and white tile. It wasn't at all like the dingy shops where I lived, with flypaper hanging from the ceiling, the floor all grimy, and the sweets in tins all open so anyone could put their dirty hand in. Mr. Poppy was a little man, skinny with bright red cheeks and white hair and always a pair of glasses slipping down to the end of his nose. He looked a bit like an elf and he was always smiling. But today as we passed his shop he was leaning in the doorway trying to smile and tears were rolling down those thin red cheeks.

We walked past Clapton Pond where the ducks were still swimming, completely unaware of the drama so close by. We walked past the little sub post office and the lady who ran it waved, then past the fire station which our class once visited, and I wondered if the firemen would soon be putting out fires from bombs. I asked Sadie and she started to cry.

We got to the station, and 'Sergeant-Major' Harris shouted, "Halt, girls!" We stopped, we waited, and we turned our heads and looked across the street. There were our Mums. We waved, we threw kisses, we cried.

And then we went through the booking office onto the platform and waited again, this time for a train that would take us who knew where.

Now, what a lot of noise! Everyone was confused, unhappy, excited. No one knew what to expect. No one knew what to do.

Then above the noise we heard the chug-chug of the train approaching. The station darkened and, with a screech of wheels, the train stopped. Miss Harris herded us into compartments, each class split up between two or three.

We sat trembling.

Finally, the whistle wailed and doors slammed, and we were off. Some of us sat and stared out of the windows. Some pulled out their lunches right away and started to eat because they were so nervous. Some started to cry, and some were laughing in a nervous, hysterical sort of way. It was a mixture of everything.

I looked at Sadie and pulled at her sleeve.

"Sadie," I said, "do you think we'll ever see our Mums again? Do you think we'll ever come back to London again? Do you think we'll die in the country?"

Sadie threw her arms around my neck.

"Oh, Kitty," she said, "don't ever leave me. Promise we'll always be together!" And she huddled close.

Exhausted from the tension of these last weeks, we looked out of the window, not knowing what else to say or do. The train chug-chugged through this sunny day. We saw the back gardens of little houses with their grey sooty roofs, and washing hanging on the lines. There wasn't even a breeze blowing the washing about. There were no children in the gardens, and no Dads digging either. We passed some allotments, where vegetables were growing. People had been asked to plant vegetables instead of flowers that year.

Then, slowly, London was behind us and the countryside began—large flat green fields with cows grazing. Sadie and I tried playing 'Cows Up Cows Down' as we used to on trains, but we just couldn't concentrate.

The train kept on stopping at little stations, empty stations. Some even had the name blacked out, and the only words we could see there were Ladies, or Gents, or WC. Finally, the train chug-chugged to a longer stop. To me, it seemed as if we had been travelling for hours and hours, though it must have been less than two. We peered out of the window. The name of this station was not blacked out. It said Much Hadham. What a strange name! Is this where Sadie and I would live, I wondered?

Miss Harris came along and called our class only.

"We're getting out here, girls," she said. "The rest of the school will stay on the train a bit longer."

We found out later they were going to places nearby called Little Hadham, and Sawbridgeworth, and others. We wondered then if we'd ever see them again.

3

The Chosen People

MY STOMACH FELT EMPTY. It was as if there was a big hole where it used to be, although I had just finished eating all those sandwiches. And I felt horribly lonely, just like the cat on the wall.

There was the name Much Hadham in large white letters hanging from the roof of the platform. Beside the sign was a door marked WC staring me in the face. Was this the place where I would live forever and ever . . . and never see my Mum and Dad, my Uncle Yudi, and my Cousin Theresa again?

But I wouldn't show anybody how I felt. I wouldn't cry, even though tears were welling up behind my eyes and starting to sting already. I was scared that if I did cry my glasses would blur over. So, I held my head high, as my mother always said I should, and waited.

Then the voice of 'Sergeant-Major' Harris boomed out at us from the platform: "All the Hut portable girls. Out! Now!" You would think that at least she would put on some kind of soft voice. But perhaps she too was scared and she didn't want to show it either.

We got up, Sadie and I still holding hands, and we got out of the train. Once again we were counted. Wouldn't it be fun if someone had escaped, I thought, just as if we were a prison gang.

Someone had forgotten her suitcase and another her lunch box, and there was such a running in and out of the train. But finally we were all together.

The train began to slowly puff and chug, smoke billowing, on its way to Little Hadham and Sawbridge-worth. Girls were waving arms out of the train and teachers were pulling them in. We waved, and many cried, and once again I wondered if I would ever see them again.

Miss Harris hurried us along, as we began the walk into the town. We crossed the footbridge over the tracks. How sleepy the little town looked as we marched down the main street. We passed the pub. It looked so different from the pubs I knew in London . . . or rather the pubs I'd seen in London. As my Dad never went into a pub, I never did either. It looked like pubs I'd seen in books by Charles Dickens with black beams in the ceilings. And looking through the little window panes, I could see brass all over and a fire burning in a huge grate.

We passed the general store and people were outside staring at us. I looked down at the cobblestones as we turned into the narrow road running off the High Street. It was all so clean. No litter on the ground, no orange peel or cigarette butts in the gutter. This was the country. This was Much Hadham.

At the end of that street was the church. Being Jewish, I had never been into a church. Would we have to go in there? It made me feel awful just to think about it. But then I saw that we were going past the church into the parish hall right behind it. Thank you God, I said to myself in relief.

We were marched into a large room with high sloping ceilings, and bare wooden floors, dark and sombre, like out of a fairy tale. At one end of the room I could see ladies pouring cups of tea and laying out currant cake. It was crowded with people, Mums, Dads, but of course not ours, on one side. And we were seated on low benches against the wall on the other. First we were given tea and cake. And then the "fun" began.

We're really going to be the Chosen People, I thought. That's how I felt. The villagers were here to choose whom they wanted without knowing a thing about us. I remember Sheila Foster was chosen first, I bet because she was so pretty. I was always secretly jealous of her. She had long blond curls and no glasses, and I had always worn glasses. She was very clever, and even in her school uniform she always looked like she was going to a party. Then Madeleine Levine was chosen. She wasn't pretty at all, but she was talking and laughing with all the Mums and Dads.

Sadie and I sat and sat, huddled together on that bench along the wall. Finally, when almost everyone had been chosen, two people walked toward us—a big, blonde lady with her hair pulled back, and a shorter man. The Young Couple: that's what my Mum would call them later when she came to visit. They looked at Sadie and me sitting there all forlorn, and pointed and said, "We'll take these two."

My stomach turned over and I held onto Sadie tighter, and we got up and followed the Young Couple.

We told them our names, even though our labels were pinned on our coats. They took us by the hand and we carried our case in the other, and began the walk to what they called their little cottage which they said was about two miles outside the village.

It was beginning to get dark by this time. So the Lady took our hands, and the Gentleman took our cases. The road was very straight. And we were so tired. But not actually knowing where we were going kept us alert.

We passed only one house along the narrow road. It was set well back so we couldn't hear anybody there. We only saw some dim light coming from it, and smelled cows even before we heard them mooing. The rest of the way was dark and silent and I wondered if we'd be ending up in a witch's den. I couldn't even talk to Sadie about it because the Lady and the Gentleman would hear.

After what seemed like a long time we came to their place. Such a long way from a neighbour. So different from our street at home, where I could look into the next yard if my Dad lifted me up over the fence. And I always saw my neighbours, leaning out of their front windows calling to their children in the street.

How different all this was!

Theirs was a little two-storey cottage. And as we came in the front door, there was a strange smell like that of a candle that had just gone out. The place was very dark and the Gentleman struck a match to a large lamp on a table.

"What's that funny smell?" I asked.

"It's paraffin from the lamp," he said. "We have no gas or electricity. This is the only light we have."

I had never seen a place like this before, not even in books. There was an armchair, some wooden chairs, a little polished table, and a carpet on the rough wooden floor. The place was tiny, but so clean. And it seemed to me that the whole room was dominated by an enormous paraffin lamp sitting on the table. This was the only light so all the rest of the room was in darkness. Shadows were playing on the walls and ceiling. It was so eerie. We were scared. Imagine, coming from a city where the houses are so close together that I could see into the boy next door's bedroom, and now here, living miles from anyplace and anyone, in a really spooky house.

Still the Young Couple tried to put us at ease. Sadie and I squeezed together in the big armchair near the lamp so that we could be together when the shadows pressed down on us, and we kind of comforted each other.

The Lady gave us some milk and a sandwich and said we would have to sleep upstairs, on the floor.

The first difficulty was the sandwich. It looked wonderful, but when I took the first bite, I knew it was something I was not allowed to eat.

I asked her what the sandwich was, and she said it was a nice ham sandwich. Again my heart sank. What was I going to do now? I looked at Sadie. I saw she was about to cry.

"Excuse me," I said. "We're Jewish, and we mustn't

eat ham, or any meat that isn't kosher. Could we have something else?"

The Lady looked at me wide-eyed, and I saw creases form on her forehead. I don't think she understood what I meant. But she went into the kitchen and the Gentleman followed right after her.

"Kitty, what shall we do?" Sadie whispered.

"Shush," I said. "Let's try and hear what they're saying."

We strained our ears, and we heard, " . . . don't understand . . . cheese and jam . . . ask them later."

What a relief I felt when I heard her busy getting another sandwich for us. And it was good. They sat down opposite us, and the Gentleman asked us about our school.

"It's an all-girls' school."

"And most of the girls are Jewish . . . but not the teachers, of course."

"And it's a long way from where we live. We have to come by tram."

"Both Sadie and I keep kosher. We were sure we'd have trouble about this . . . coming to the country without our parents. We've never eaten in a non-Jewish home. We knew we'd have to out here. But we would never eat meat. We thought we could eat around it . . . "

"What's kosher?" the Gentleman asked. Sadie and I looked at each other.

"Well," I said, "it's meat that's been killed in a special way and that's all we eat in our house. And it can't be ham or pork or anything like that."

Whether he understood I really don't know, but I was thankful at least that Sadie and I were on the same level Jewishly. We would get through this together.

Afterwards, they took us up the rickety wooden stairs to a little room with a mattress on the floor by the window. The rest of the room was bare and dark except for the moonlight shining through the little panes.

It was very nice of these people to take us in. They didn't even have a proper bed for us. But everyone in the country, we were told, was asked to billet children who came from London and other big cities, because the government was so sure that this was going to be a terrible war, and all the big cities would be bombed right away.

Anyway, we went to bed feeling very lonely and very abandoned. We cried ourselves to sleep.

4

The Siren Sounds

WE SLEPT HEAVILY that night. We had cried and cried ourselves to sleep. And so when sleep did come, it was deep but fitful.

We woke to the sun pouring through our little window. But when we opened our eyes there were two pairs of eyes staring down at us.

It was the Young Couple. What were they doing standing over us like that?

"What are you looking at us like that for?" I whispered. "Have we done something wrong?"

"Of course not! We're just looking for the horns."

"Horns!" we burst out together.

"We were always told that Jews had horns and you're the first Jews we've ever seen," the Gentleman said quietly.

"Yes. When you told us you were Jewish, we looked for the horns," the Lady added. "We couldn't see them when you were awake. So we thought we'd be able to see them when you were sleeping."

"That's daft," I said. "We don't have horns. We're just the same as everybody else!"

And we laughed! And they laughed! And they told us to come down for breakfast.

She had made fresh bread that we had with thick creamy butter fresh from the farm and lots of lovely homemade strawberry jam. Afterwards, she made us write a postcard to our Mums, to tell them where we were, and invite them to visit the following Saturday.

Then the Young Couple took us out for a walk through the fields. We had been to the country before, of course. But only to the seaside, like Southend or Westcliff. It was always crowded there, with lots of children running about and making sandcastles.

But this country was so different. There were great big fields with horses meandering about. We were scared of them at first. But the Young Couple introduced us to them. They knew every one by name. They showed us how to feed them sugar from our hand. They taught us the names of different plants, and showed us a birds' nest that had fallen to the ground, with some tiny blue eggs still in it. But the nicest part of the day was lying in the tall grass, listening to insects singing, and stretching blades of grass between our thumbs and whistling through them.

After lunch they showed us how to get back to the village and the Parish Hall where we had been told we had to meet each day. We were so excited to see our class again. We all wanted to know where everyone was staying. Some were happy. They told us they were staying in lovely homes. Good old Sheila Foster was in the best of the lot, of course. But Pam Lazarus was staying over the pub. And Jean Godfrey was in a little cottage just like ours down another long lane. How excitedly we talked about the strangeness of it all!

We got home just in time for supper. And as it got dark, we were sent to bed. We could see the paraffin lamp flickering downstairs. We talked and talked. We wondered when we would see our Mums and Dads. On Saturday, we hoped. Worried, unhappy, and very homesick, we fell asleep.

We exploded awake to the terrible wail of an air raid siren. It was already morning. It was a sound we had heard before, in practice drills. But now it seemed to go on forever.

My stomach turned over. It must be war. And I could almost hear my Uncle Yudi carrying on to my Mum saying, "I told you so, Passie. I told you Chamberlain sold us out to the bloody Germans. I always said this would happen."

I grabbed Sadie. And we clung together.

"What do we do?"

"Where do we go?"

"Where's our Mum and Dad?"

"Let's go home," I said. "Right now."

"We can't."

"I want to go home."

"You can't. You have to stay here"

"I don't care. I've got two shillings. Stay if you want. I'm getting a half fare and going home."

"You can't. Your Mum said you have to stay with me."

And we sobbed, and clung to each other.

The Young Couple came running up the stairs. They tried to comfort us. She held us close.

"It's all right. You'll be safe with us. As long as the war is on, we'll look after you."

They stayed with us until the all-clear sounded. We hadn't heard any airplanes, or bombs. Later they walked us to the Parish Hall. They didn't have a wireless. They too wanted to know for sure if the war had started. And it had. They told us when we got there. It was September 3, 1939. We were all so nervous. Miss Harris tried to calm us down.

"The country is safe, girls," she said. "That's why we're here. For the next two weeks, there'll be no school. Just enjoy the country. But don't stray too far. And report to the Parish Hall every day as usual, for instructions."

And that's what we did.

We roamed the fields, played hide and seek, and rolled in the long grass and felt the corn prickles on our legs. We fed the horses and went to the farm up the road to watch the cows being milked. Everything was so beautiful, so different from what we had known.

But all we thought of, and longed for, was Saturday. The week seemed to go on forever.

5

The Visit

WOULD SATURDAY ever come? It seemed such a long way away.

The Young Couple talked about the war. But as they didn't have a wireless, they had to get their news from the people around them.

We wanted to know if London had been bombed yet. We nagged them to find out. But nobody had heard anything.

So, we worried. Would there be bombs before next Saturday? Would our parents be able to come? The thought of them not coming gave me a hole in my stomach that seemed to get deeper as the week went on. Sometimes it was even hard to swallow. And I often felt sick.

But we got through it, somehow. We walked a lot, Sadie and I, or played with other girls. But by dusk we were back helping the Lady put up blackout curtains she was making for the whole cottage.

Finally, Friday night was here. We couldn't wait until morning. In bed, Sadie and I talked about the strange week: barns covered with leaves, lorries covered with leaves and branches. Sometimes we couldn't tell what was field and what was camouflage. But we went to sleep full of plans for the next day.

Right after breakfast, the waiting began. We couldn't settle down. We kept running up to the road and back. It seemed hours, but suddenly we saw three specks coming along from Much Hadham.

"It must be them," I screamed.

"It has to be them," yelled Sadie.

We ran up that long straight road, nearly tripping several times.

"Sadie," I said. "They're alive. They haven't been killed by the bombs. They're really here."

There was my Mum, in the same grey three-quarter coat she had worn at the station. Her crinkly hair was pulled back just as I remembered.

Nothing had changed.

She kissed me over and over, both of us crying away.

"Daddy couldn't come," she said, sniffling into her hankie. "He tried to get off. You know he's making army huts. And they need them badly now. But he sent a letter for you."

Sadie's Mum and Dad hugged and kissed her, too. Mrs. Davidovitch was a little round woman, her Dad taller but very skinny, with straight hair. I wondered why I always notice someone's hair. Maybe it was because I had so much of it, and it was so unruly. That's why everyone called me Mrs. Mop.

We hugged one another and felt so good.

We walked to the cottage where the Young Couple was waiting for us, and introduced them as our foster parents as we had been told to. How we filled up their tiny front room, and how strange it seemed to see our parents in this place.

(Later, my Mum told me how upset she was when she heard me say 'foster parents'. To her it meant that these strangers would look after me for the rest of my life if anything happened to her. But at that moment she didn't let on how she felt.)

Our parents had brought presents for the Young Couple. My Mum had a tin of boiled sweets for them. But Sadie's parents had brought lovely fabric. Mr. Davidovitch was a master tailor and made suits for men and women. What a wonderful present, I thought. But it made me feel bad. I felt poor next to Sadie. But that was all my Mum could afford.

We all went outside for a picnic on the lush grass of the field next to the cottage. Our Mums had brought sandwiches and the Young Couple gave us something to drink.

And then . . . the question we'd been waiting for:

"How are you managing, Kitty? Are you eating everything?"

Before I could answer Sadie's Dad chimed in, "You know you must eat everything—even if it isn't kosher."

"Make sure you don't make a mess," added Mrs. Davidovitch. "Keep everything tidy. And don't answer them back!"

"We couldn't eat ham," I said.

"It made us feel sick," said Sadie.

"But they're ever so nice," I said. "They gave us some cheese instead. They don't know anything about kosher. But when we told them, it was all right."

The two Mums stared at each other.

Then, to change the subject, we took them to the farm next door, and showed them all the things we'd seen and done that week.

My Mum told me about the funny things my little Uncle Yudi was doing training to be an air raid warden. We laughed and talked until it was time to say goodbye. And then more tears.

"We'll see you soon."

"Don't worry."

"London is very quiet."

"There aren't any bombs."

And they were off. How long would it be till we saw them again?

6
Moving On

THE NEXT DAY when we went to the Parish Hall, Miss Harris told us that we would all be moving on Saturday to a market town nearby as there were no schools for us in Much Hadham.

"Enjoy the rest of the week, girls. And try to make friends with the local children."

We did try. But every time we approached them, they would poke out their tongues at us and run away. Maybe they too thought we had horns.

Saturday came too soon, and it was time to move on. The Young Couple walked us to the Parish Hall holding our cases, and holding our hands.

There were buses waiting. We said goodbye to the Young Couple and promised to write. But this goodbye wasn't awful at all, not like the goodbyes in London. It was just a wave . . . and a wondering what would happen next.

Miss Harris told us that Bishop Stortford was where we were going. It wasn't far, she said, and before long we were in front of another Parish Hall. Inside was the rest of the school from the other nearby villages. There were benches all around as before, and the same Lysol smell, and Sadie and I huddled together once again on a bench wondering who would choose us now. But this time I felt I wasn't alone on that wall . . . even if it took ages for us to be chosen. There was Sheila Foster first off and

Madie Levine second off just as before. Sadie and I kept on smiling in the hope that someone would choose us early. But it took a long time.

Just when I'd almost given up, a lady and gentleman pointed to us and came over. He was tall, with a large moustache, pink cheeks, and twinkling eyes. He wore a country suit, tweedy, rough, and warm-looking. The lady was shorter, with a face like a full moon, and straight yellow hair pulled back. But she didn't look as cheery as he. They looked at the tags on our coats.

"Kitty Simmonds. Sadie Da-vi-dov-itch," she said. "Oh, Eric." And she turned to her husband. "Not an English name. Where do you come from, then?" she asked.

"I'm from London," Sadie said, looking at me.

"All right. All right. Never mind. We're Mr. and Mrs. Barker. You're to come home with us."

They took our cases and held our hands and led us outside to a big car. We got in, while Mr. Barker put our cases in the boot.

"It's not far to our house, ducks," Mr. Barker said. "Just up the road past the post office." We giggled.

"Aren't we lucky," I whispered. "We got a couple with a car. Sadie, this is going to be fun."

"We don't have any children, I'm afraid," Mr. Barker said. "But we've got a nice big house. And for our war effort, we thought we'd take some evacuees. We think you'll do nicely."

"Especially London evacuees," Mrs. Barker chimed

in. "Everyone says London's going to be bombed any day."

I grabbed Sadie and we clung together. We didn't say another word the rest of the way.

The car stopped outside a house with a low hedge. Mrs. Barker led us through an iron gate up the path to the front door. She unlocked the door and we stepped into a gleaming passage, with a lovely carpet on the shiny floor. A carpeted staircase with brass rods on each step and a polished banister led upstairs. Beside it stood a fancy table with a glass bowl full of flowers. Everything smelled of polish and lemon, not of cows and cats as before.

"So, here we are," Mr. Barker said. "Come along. I'll take your cases upstairs and show you your room."

"Show them where the bathroom is, Eric," Mrs. Barker called after us. "Wash your hands, girls, and come straight down for tea."

Our room was lovely. Two beds, with a table and a little carpet in between, and curtains on the window. Nothing at all like Much Hadham.

And the bathroom! It wasn't outside, like my house in London, but on the same landing as our bedroom, with a chain, and proper paper, not newspaper, to wipe.

How lucky could we be!

But I thought of my Mum, all alone in our cold house ... nothing like this ... and I wanted to be there even so. Tears began to come. Sadie would think I was daft if I told her how I felt. So I tried to hide it.

In the kitchen the Barkers were sitting at a big white

wooden table laid for tea, with thin little sandwiches and sickly little cakes.

"I'm the town baker, you know," Mr. Barker said. "So you'll have lots of treats like this . . . as long as there's no sugar rationing."

"Now, Eric, you'll make the girls sick."

It was a lovely tea. We told them about our families and our school. Afterwards Mrs. Barker sent us up to bed.

"Don't forget to pull the blackout curtains before you switch on the light!" she said. Ha! No paraffin lamps here.

The next morning we were shaken gently awake by Mrs. Barker. When we opened our eyes, we didn't know for a second where we were. Mrs. Barker smiled down.

"Hurry girls. Get up and come down for breakfast. It's almost time for church, and with war declared there should be a good sermon."

The sun poured into the room. And we looked out the window onto the back garden.

"Look, Sadie," I said. "There are rows and rows of plants down there. Must be vegetables Mr. Barker has planted for the war effort."

"We'll have plenty of fresh greens here," Sadie said. "Not like the rotten stuff our Mums have to buy in the market down the Lane."

Again, the table was laid, and Mr. and Mrs. Barker were all dressed up in their Sunday best.

"Eat up girls. Just a quick breakfast. Or we'll be late for church," she said.

"Oh, thank you," I said. "But we can't go with you."

"Why ever not?" Mrs. Barker asked. "Everyone in Bishop Stortford goes to church on Sunday morning."

"Well, we're Jewish. We don't go to church. Maybe there's a synagogue nearby," I said, "and we'll go there."

"Except it's Sunday," Sadie said, "and synagogue is only on Saturdays."

"Jewish?" Mrs. Barker said. "They didn't tell us that! Well, we haven't time to talk about it now. We have to go. If you're staying home you can wash up and get the kitchen clean for lunch. Come on, Eric!"

We heard the back door close. Here we were, all alone in this beautiful house. We wanted to look around, explore every nook and cranny, but we were afraid they'd come home early and catch us.

"Have you ever done any washing up?" I asked Sadie. "My Mum wouldn't ever let me. She always threw me out of the kitchen. She said the kitchen was too small for the two of us."

"Me too," Sadie said.

"Well," I said, "I think we'd better start. There's a basin in the sink already."

"Do we wash with hot water or cold?"

"Hot, I suppose. We'd better put a kettle on."

"But look, there are two taps over the sink. Maybe one is hot and one is cold. Let's try."

I turned on one tap and the water was warm.

"Look," I said, "I'll wash and you wipe. But be ever so careful not to drop anything. I wouldn't want to get on the wrong side of her."

It was slow going. But finally we finished.

"I don't think we should put the plates away," Sadie said. "We'll just put them on the side. The cupboards are so high. We'd have to stand on a chair to find the right place."

It was a lovely bright kitchen, with shiny copper pots hanging from the walls.

"Look, Sadie. They even have a larder," I said, opening a door. There were shelves and shelves of food: bread, butter and jam, and bottles and tins filled with fruit.

"We won't go hungry here," Sadie said.

We sat down at the table to wait for the Barkers to come back. By now, the room was filled with a delicious smell. Mrs. Barker had left the Sunday dinner in the oven to keep warm. It wasn't the smell of chicken soup or cholent but it still smelled good.

I thought about Sunday dinner.

"What are we going to do about the meat, Sadie?" I said. "The same as in Much Hadham?"

"Yes," Sadie said.

"Your Dad said we have to eat everything. But I couldn't eat their meat, Sadie. I'd die."

"Me too," Sadie said. "We'll eat around it. We'll eat the greens and potatoes. And if there's sweets that will be enough. And we won't tell our parents."

Just then the Barkers came home.

"I see the washing up's done. Thanks dears. Now let's

lay the table for dinner," Mrs. Barker said.

"You girls really missed a treat this morning," she went on. "The minister gave a marvelous sermon . . . all about the war. Everybody has to help do their bit. He even spoke about you evacuees. He said you all should be grateful and help your foster parents. There were lots of children from your school there, you know. I still can't understand why you didn't come."

We all sat down, and Mr. Barker said Grace. We listened, and lowered our eyes as they did, and even said Amen.

Mr. Barker carved the joint and Mrs. Barker served the rest.

It did look nice.

"How's the joint, Eric?" Mrs. Barker said.

"Just right, my dear. Nice and juicy. And the Yorkshire is delicious. Now dig in, girls. This is Mrs. B.'s specialty."

We began to eat our vegetables and Yorkshire.

"How's the meat, girls?"

"I'm sorry, Mr. Barker," I said, raising my eyes, "but we can't eat the meat."

"What!? Can't eat the meat?" Mrs. Barker exclaimed. "You'll not waste good food, not in my house."

"But you see we only eat kosher meat. We're Jewish, like we told you," I said.

"We'll eat everything else," Sadie said. "We don't want to be difficult, but we just can't eat the meat."

"Kosher? What's kosher?" Mrs. Barker said. "I've

never heard of that word. I don't know what you're talking about."

"Look girls," Mr. Barker said. "We took you in to save you from the bombs. And when you're in our house you'll do what we say and eat what we eat. That's flat."

Tears welled up.

"We don't want to be trouble," I said. "But we just can't eat your meat. If there's ever rationing, you can have all of ours!"

We ate the rest of the meal in complete silence.

Then came the washing up. Only this time Mrs. Barker put everything away. "They're my best dishes," she said. She was taller than us so she didn't need to stand on a chair to reach the cupboards.

As we put the chairs back in place around the table, she pulled one chair back out.

"What's this dirt on here?" she asked, glaring at us.

"Well, Mrs. Barker," I said, "we stood on the chair to try to put the plates away this morning. But even then we couldn't reach. The cupboards are so high up. So we left them on the side."

"You take your shoes off next time you stand on a chair in my house . . . even if you don't do that in your house!"

We looked down at the floor. "Is that all, now, Mrs. Barker?" I asked. "Can we go outside for a bit?"

"Well, all right. But don't get lost. And be back before blackout, you hear!"

I took Sadie's hand, and we went out the back door.

7

The Barkers

THANK GOODNESS we're out of there," I said to Sadie when the door closed behind us. "Now I feel free, don't you?"

Sadie agreed.

"Let's see if we can find some of the other girls," she said. "I wonder where they are? Do you think we should go back in and ask her?"

"Well, I won't go back in there unless I have to," I said. "She's such a misery. Let's go and look at the town. Maybe we'll meet some of the girls."

So we wandered toward the town, looking in the shop windows. We couldn't go in, of course, as it was Sunday. We saw lots of children playing on the streets, but none of our girls. Some of the children stared at us in our school uniforms, and I heard one say to another, "Look! Evacuees!"

It began to drizzle. The town looked grey.

"I think we'd better go back, Sadie," I said. "We don't want her starting on us again."

It wasn't hard finding our way back. And it wasn't even dark yet when we knocked. Mr. Barker let us in.

"Glad you're back in time for tea," he said. "Mrs. Barker was just wondering where you were, weren't you, dear?"

Mrs. Barker just continued laying the table. "From now on, girls," she said, "use the back door. The front door is only for visitors."

We sat down to a high tea of sandwiches, egg with watercress, and sardines. Thank goodness no meat, I thought.

"Not much cake today, dears. But tomorrow there'll be more. Have to get to work right after tea," Mr. Barker said. "Got to get the bread ready for the morning, you know. Been doing my allotment all afternoon. Got to get those potatoes and onions dug up for the winter . . . to help with the war effort, eh, Gladys?"

Mrs. Barker nodded.

"Been a baker all m'life, you know, girls. M'father before me, he taught me the trade. Don't know who's going to take over when I'm gone though. Should've had m'own children years ago."

"Don't talk like that, Eric," Mrs. Barker said sharply. "You just enjoy what you're doing."

Mr. Barker wanted to talk more, but whenever he started to talk about himself, Mrs. Barker shut him up.

We were glad when tea was over, and hurried with the washing up so we could leave the room. This time we took off our shoes when we stood on the chair.

On the way up to our room, we heard Mrs. Barker's nagging voice: "Pull the blackout curtains before you switch on the light, girls."

She didn't have to tell us. We knew we had to do it anyway.

"Sadie," I said, "do you think it will be all right here?"

"I don't know," she said, "but we have to make the

best of it, don't we? You don't like her, do you?"

"No. But he's all right . . . when she lets him. Wish she would go to work and he would stay home, don't you? But we'd better not talk about them too much. They may hear . . . and then there'll be trouble."

"C'mon," Sadie said, "let's try that lovely bathroom again."

We hurried off together, washed, cleaned our teeth, and took a long time looking at ourselves in the big glass.

"Just think," I said. "We don't have to go outside to the lav. And it's so nice and warm when you sit down." And we giggled.

We got into our pajamas, and went back to our room. We talked a bit and read a bit and, when we heard the Barkers coming up the stairs, quickly switched off the light.

8

On Our Own

THE NEXT DAY after breakfast we met, as we had been told to, at the Herts and Essex Girls' School.

We expected to start school that morning. But when the teachers were finally able to get us in order, Dr. Hunt, our headmistress, had a surprise for us.

"Good morning, girls," she said. "I hope you're happy in your new homes. However, I have to tell you that school is not going to start today. We are arranging for the Stortford girls to come to school in the morning, and we Londoners will come in the afternoon. But that doesn't mean you'll have less work. It means you'll have more homework, which I know you'll want to do to keep up the high standard of our school. Your teachers will give you a note from me to your foster parents. School will start on Wednesday. You'll come at one o'clock and leave at four. Your teachers will now call your names and show you where your classes are. Now, girls, I expect you always to be on your best behaviour. You're guests of the town of Bishop Stortford. Don't let them have any complaints."

On the way to see our room, Pamela said, "Why we all can't be together I dunno."

"Perhaps they think we have some kind of disease," Madie Levine joined in.

"Maybe it's because we come from the slums," I said.

"Maybe they think we have fleas," Sadie said.

We often saw Stortford girls in their uniforms. They would stare at us, and were never friendly.

"It's all right," Sadie would say, "we have each other, so why should we care!"

But I really wanted to make friends.

We also hoped that Miss Harris would come to visit us. But she never did. I suppose she thought we were happy.

We did tell her about the meat. She said that when school started things would be different, and some kind of arrangement would be made for us.

So, for the next two days, we explored the town.

Bishop Stortford was not so bad. It was more city than country. There were lots of shops, even a Woolworth's, and a picture palace, and best of all a fish and chip shop.

"So what shall we do now?" I said to Sadie as we left school.

"Let's go find Mr. Barker's shop," Sadie suggested. "He said it was in the High Street."

We had no trouble finding it. A great big sign was hanging over the door, E. Barker, Baker. We pressed our noses to the window. A girl was serving behind the counter. The smell of cakes coming out of that door made my mouth water.

"Come on, Sadie," I said. "Let's go in."

We waited our turn. "Can we please speak to Mr. Barker?" Sadie asked. "We're his evacuees."

She called him, and he came out. He looked surprised when he saw us. He was covered with flour—his undershirt was splashed with flour, the top of his hat was full of flour, and there was even a smudge of flour at the end of his nose. This was not the Mr. Barker we knew in the house, all proper in his nice tweed suit. Here he was all floury, but nice somehow . . . like an Irish leprechaun, with a smile on his face.

"Hello, hello, girls! What are you doing here?"

"We don't start school till Wednesday," I said. "So, we thought we'd try to find your shop. Can we come to the back to see how you do your baking?"

He thought for a bit.

"Well," he said, "if you don't tell the missus. Come in. Come in."

He led us into a big square room with black iron ovens against one wall, and enormous bowls of dough all over the place. An old man was at one table punching down a great big mound of dough. He huffed and puffed as he limped from one table to the next. It must have been a hard job.

"These are my war effort, Jock," Mr. Barker said. Jock gave us a quick nod and went on huffing and punching.

"Can we try that, Jock?" I asked.

"Sorry, miss. The guv'n'r won't allow that." And he looked at Mr. Barker.

As we watched, he shaped bits of dough into buns that looked like they belonged on the top of Dr. Hunt's head. She wore her hair just like that.

Then we saw him take out a great big tray of treacle tarts from one of the ovens. Mmmm . . . that smell! We couldn't take our eyes off them. I think Mr. Barker saw us eyeing them. But he didn't say anything.

All this time Mr. Barker was singing as he helped Jock punch and shape loaves. He seemed so happy, not like he was at home. He never sang there.

"Now, run along girls. And promise me you won't tell the missus. She doesn't like me to have visitors in the shop, especially in the back."

But as we left, he gave us each a hot treacle tart. "Just a little treat for you both . . . . And oh yes, before you go, I must tell you, tomorrow is market day. Somehow I don't think you'll have seen anything like it before. The farmers bring their animals to be auctioned. You go and see tomorrow. It'll be a real treat for you. Starts early though. So you'd better go right after breakfast."

We went the next morning. It was bright and sunny. Each animal had a tag around its neck. The larger animals were put in stalls, and the small ones—sheep, lambs, and pigs—were in pens. He was right. We'd never seen anything like this before. The sheep were so wooly. The lambs were jumping all over one another. And the pigs were grunting away, not seeming to care what happened.

When everything was ready, the animals were brought out one by one, and the bidding began. There was lots of shouting as bids went higher and higher. And when there was silence, the auctioneer would shout "Going, going, gone" and slam his hammer down on the table, and the new owner would lead the animal to his cart.

The first time it happened I said to Sadie, "Look, it's got a tag around its neck. Just like us. Except we were given away, not sold." Did Sadie ever laugh!

It was an exciting morning. The only thing we hated about it all was the smell. But the fun of it was worth those horrid smells. My Mum said later, when we told her about it, that it was a healthy smell. Yeech.

9

Goodbye Mrs. Prior

ONE DAY, AS WE WERE getting ready for lunch, we heard a terrible crash downstairs. We quickly ran down and saw Mrs. Prior, the old lady who kept the house so clean and shiny, flat on her back in the passage, with the little table and the flower vase that was on it scattered over the floor. Mrs. Barker was leaning over her.

Poor Mrs. Prior. We didn't know what had happened but we heard her saying, "Bloody floor. I knew I'd kill m'self on it one day."

And Mrs. Barker was saying, "It's all right, Mrs. Prior. You've only slipped."

"Crikey," said Mrs. Prior. "Only slipped! I could've broked m'bleedin' neck." And she burst into tears.

Mrs. Barker helped her up and sat her on the stairs. Sadie picked up the fallen table, and I the broken vase. There was water all over the floor. The flowers had been trodden in.

"Go put on the kettle, Kitty," Mrs. Barker said, "and make a cup of tea. And strong now."

I went towards the kitchen. Mrs. Prior was snivelling and I could hear her mumbling, "Bloody 'ell! All that bloody polish. 'Oo cares if the place doesn't shine?"

"Now, now," Mrs. Barker said. "Have a nice strong cup of tea and you'll be right as rain again."

"I'm leavin', Mrs. Barker! Do ya 'ear?" Mrs. Prior went on. "I don't want your bloody tea. I want me money.

I'm not workin' 'ere any more. I can get a better job in munitions."

She got up, found her coat in the cupboard, and put her scarf over her head.

"Can I have me money now, 'cause I'm bloody well not comin' back."

"Come, Mrs. Prior. Have a strong cup of tea and you'll feel better," Mrs. Barker said, trying to coax Mrs. Prior to sit down.

"I told ya I don't want your tea. I'm leavin', you 'ear. And I want me money now!"

"Come for it tonight, Mrs. Prior, when Mr. Barker comes home. I'm sure you'll feel differently about it then."

"Oh no, dearie. If you don't give me m'money now, I'll just sit 'ere till you do." And she sat back down and stared straight at Mrs. Barker.

Finally, Mrs. Barker went into the kitchen, got the money, and gave it to her. Mrs. Prior stalked out, nearly tripping on the door mat as she went, slamming the door behind her.

Sadie and I wanted to giggle, but we didn't dare.

"What are you going to do now?" Sadie asked.

"I don't know yet," Mrs. Barker replied. "Kitty, go inside and get a rag, and wipe up this water. Sadie, pick up the flowers."

She had a strange look on her face just then.

When I came back with the rag, Sadie had already cleared away the flowers.

While I was working, Mrs. Barker said, "You know,

girls, it's very hard to get help these days. Everyone's in the army, it seems. I think it would be a good idea if you two helped with the housework from now on. You're only going to school afternoons. So you can do some housework mornings and do your homework after school. That's a good idea. I'm sure Mr. Barker will agree to that."

Sadie and I looked at each other.

"But we've never done housework," I said. "We don't have floors like this at home. We wouldn't know what to do."

"Don't worry," she said. "I'll show you. It'll do you both good to learn these things. Now let's have a cup of tea before I make lunch. Can't waste a good pot of tea, girls!"

After lunch we couldn't wait to get out and talk about it all.

"We'll see what happens," Sadie said. "If it's awful, we'll tell Miss Harris. And I'm sure Mr. Barker won't let us work hard. He's so nice."

10

Charring

NOTHING WAS SAID about Mrs. Prior at tea that night.

"What kind of a day did you have, girls?" Mr. Barker asked.

"Oh, lovely," we giggled.

"How was your day, Eric?" Mrs. Barker asked.

"Same as usual," he replied. "Nothing different." And he gave us a big wink when Mrs. Barker wasn't looking.

I wanted to giggle again.

We just talked about nothing! Nothing about Mrs. Prior, nothing about housework, even though she said she would discuss it with him when he came home.

After tea we went up to our room.

"Sadie," I said. "She said she was going to talk to him about it."

"Don't be daft," Sadie said. "She's not going to talk to him in front of us, is she now?"

"Maybe you're right," I said. "But do you think he'll stick up for us?"

Suddenly we heard loud voices. The Barkers were having a row, or that's what it sounded like to us. The kitchen door must have been open. We crept out onto the landing, and sat huddled together on the top step, straining to hear.

"Gladys," Mr. Barker was saying, "how can you do such a thing? Those poor little mites! How can you expect them to do charring?"

"Listen here, Eric," she said. "Mrs. Prior packed it in, and those two can make up for one Mrs. Prior."

"They're only mites, Glad. You'll get yourself into trouble. We said we'd take them in. We'd didn't say we'd make them char for us."

"Eric, you look after your shop and I'll look after my

house. They'll do what I think is best. I'm not going on my hands and knees any more. And this way they can pay their way."

"Gladys . . . "

"Enough, Eric. That's enough! Let's not hear any more about it."

We heard her push back her chair. We scurried into our room and closed the door.

"Blimey, can you believe that? He tried to stick up for us. And she told him off every time," I said.

The next morning, we made our beds as usual, had our breakfast, did the washing up, and then things began to happen. Mrs. Barker told us that from now on we'd have to sweep the kitchen floor first thing. "And mind you get into all the corners. And then you can sweep up the larder," she said.

Sadie said she would do that, but after a bit, she asked me to come and help.

"There's so many things in the way," she said, " I can't get into the corners."

That larder! It was a big square cupboard off the kitchen that you could walk into, with shelves all around where they kept cakes, flour, sugar, fruit and vegetables. When we came in, we had to change our shoes and leave the ones from outside on the larder floor. We never took our shoes off at home, just wiped them on the mat at the front door. But here, everything was different. We had to keep our satchels on the larder floor, too. We didn't think our satchels would make a mess. And it seemed so funny to keep shoes and satchels in the same place as food and cakes.

That larder was hard to clean. But we finally managed. We even found a mousetrap in one corner. We didn't like that.

Mrs. Barker stood over us the whole time and told us that if we hurried we'd be free after lunch.

As soon as we finished the kitchen and the larder, she took us to do the dining room. There were all kinds of ornaments around the room, and a brass bowl full of fresh flowers on the huge polished table. The room sparkled from the sun pouring through the windows. The furniture didn't look dusty to us, but she said it had to be dusted whether it was dusty or not. She showed us how to do it.

"Now, mind, girls," she said. "Be careful of these ornaments. If you break any, you'll have to replace them."

That made us really nervous!

We never ate in this room. Mrs. Barker said it was only used for special occasions, like funerals and Christmas, I supposed.

We didn't mind the dusting, but polishing the furniture was something quite different. I had seen my Mum polishing our furniture at home. My Dad was a cabinet maker before he had to go to work on army huts. She would put some Mansion Polish on it and give it a quick rub over. That's how I tried to do it. But of course that wasn't good enough for Mrs. Barker.

"Use a little elbow grease, girls," she kept on saying.

"Make it really shine!"

"Mrs. Barker," I finally said. "I thought only Mums . . . or chars . . . do this."

"Don't be rude, Kitty," she said.

"But I'm not being rude. Honest. I really thought that . . ."

"Just get on with your job," she interrupted.

Sadie gave me a nudge, and I shut up.

It took a long time to dust and polish that room. And when we'd finished, Mrs. Barker said we'd do the floors tomorrow.

The next day straight after breakfast the real work began. Mrs. Barker gave us each an apron so that we wouldn't spoil our school uniforms, and a rag to kneel on.

"Now, Sadie," she said, "you start at one end of the passage, near the front door, and Kitty, you start at the kitchen door. And you'll meet in the middle. It'll be quicker that way, I think. Just a little bit of Mansion, mind, smear it over. And don't forget the corners. And then take a fresh cloth, here it is, and rub it in till the floor really shines. I'll lift the carpet and put it in the front room till you're finished."

She stood there with her hands on her waist, watching. She didn't even get down on her knees to show us how to do it.

It took us such a long time. When we came to the middle I stood up.

"I think it's all done, Sadie," I said. By that time Mrs.

Barker had gone to the kitchen.

"I'll go and tell her," said Sadie. "I'm sure she'll want to have a look over to see we've done it right."

But I called out, "We've finished, Mrs. Barker." She opened the kitchen door and looked down the passage.

"There's a lot of smears all over," she said. "Haven't been using much elbow grease, now, have you?"

"We're so tired," Sadie said.

"And our fingers hurt," I said.

"A little hard work won't hurt either of you," she said. "But perhaps you'll do better in the front room tomorrow. Do you want a cup o' tea now, then?"

"Please," we said.

"Go and wash your hands," she said. "And after it'll be time for lunch."

We trudged upstairs to the bathroom. "Sadie," I said, "my fingers are all sore, are yours? And my back really hurts me."

"I'm so tired," Sadie said.

"She is an old cow to make us do all this," I said. "We'll tell our Mums when they come on Sunday."

"Oh, I don't know," Sadie said. "We don't want to make trouble."

"We'll see," I said. "Let's have that cup of tea and get out of here."

11

Second Visit

WE AWOKE VERY EARLY the following Sunday morning. Thank goodness there wouldn't be any housework today. We couldn't eat our breakfast quickly enough. Our Mums had written that they would come before lunch and bring sandwiches.

We went to the station ever so early. It was deserted. But the station master told us the timetables were all mixed up that day.

"Our luck," I said. "Now they may not even come at all." I looked at Sadie. Her eyes were full of tears. My stomach was hurting.

"I think we'd better wait, anyway, just in case," Sadie said.

The stationmaster heard us. "Now ducks, it's no good you hangin' round 'ere all day. You'd better run along 'ome. They'll come if the train comes. Run along 'ome now." And he hustled us out of the waiting room.

We dawdled our way home, hoping we'd hear the train coming. Then, just before eleven, there was a knock on the door. We ran to open it, slipping over our polished floor and nearly tumbling over each other. There they were, looking exactly the same: my Mum in her grey three-quarter coat, and fat little Mrs. Davidovitch, and her skinny little husband. Mr. and Mrs. Spratt, I thought. We nearly knocked them over with our hugs and kisses.

They came into the passage and looked around.

"Oh, Kitty, what a beautiful house," my Mum exclaimed. "How lucky you are. You must be so happy here."

I burst into tears. "Oh, Mum, I've missed you so much." I could hear Sadie crying, too.

Just then Mrs. Barker came out.

"Girls, why the tears? Aren't you glad to see your parents?" She took us all into the kitchen. Mr. Barker was just putting on the kettle.

"Hello," he said. "I'm so glad to meet the parents of these lovely girls. They're a real help to us here. Cheered up the whole house. Isn't that so, Gladys?"

Mrs. Barker just nodded.

"Do sit down," Mr. Barker said. "Tea will be right up."

"We have something for you," Mrs. Davidovitch said.

Oh no, I thought, presents again. My Mum, of course, had brought boiled sweets, but this time the box was a little bigger. They were still boiled sweets, though, and I still wished she hadn't brought them. Sadie's parents had brought fabric again—tweed for Mr. Barker, just like the suit he always wore on Sundays. He loved it. And there was a length of lovely red wool for Mrs. Barker.

The Barkers were ever so friendly to the Davidovitches—because of the fabric, I supposed. I was miserable about those boiled sweets.

"You must excuse us now," Mr. Barker said. "We're off to church. But the girls will help you to some tea. They know where everything is. And then they'll want to show you their room."

"Thank you," my Mum said. "That would be very nice."

I had it all planned. We'd have tea, and show them around, and then get out and away from that hateful house for a while.

They were so happy with our room. So clean, so bright, they said, and it looked out over the garden, and the toilet was inside.

"How lucky you children are," Mr. Davidovitch said. "Bit of a difference from Stepney and all its muck. Anyway, he's a cheerful old toff. You must have a good laugh with him. But I bet she works hard keeping this place so bright and clean. Everything looks so shiny." He turned to my Mum. "And she does seem like a kind woman. Don't you think so, Mrs. Simmonds?"

"I'm not quite sure. Perhaps," my Mum answered.

Little did they know who kept this place so bright! Should I tell them, I wondered? I looked at Sadie. I could tell she felt the same. We just wanted to get out of this house. I was suffocating from all the nice things our parents were saying.

"Let's go to the market square now," I said. "We'll eat our sandwiches there, and you can see the town on the way."

We pulled them out, without having tea, promising we'd find a drink when we got there. The market square was almost deserted, just a few old men sitting on benches. We saw Pam with her Mum and Paula with hers, and we all talked together. Our Mums told theirs what a beautiful house we were living in, and how lucky we were. It made me sick to hear them. So I asked about London. They said it was quiet, no bombs, but the blackout was still on and there was talk of rationing.

"If it's quiet, Mum, why can't I come home?" I said.

"But the bombs might start any day," she said. "And what would we do then?"

"Well, if it's quiet at Christmas, can I come home for the holidays?"

"Perhaps. We'll see."

Then we told them about our trouble with the meat.

"You must make the best of it and eat everything since the Barkers are so nice to you," my Mum said.

"But how can we eat their meat?" I said. "I'll be sick if I do."

"You both make the best of it," Mrs. Davidovitch said.

I wanted to tell my Mum about the housework. I didn't know what to do. I didn't want to spoil her day. Again I felt all by myself. I wanted to tell her. I looked at Sadie, hoping that maybe she would say something. But she didn't. And I was like that lonely cat again, all by myself.

And then I thought: if we make sure our work's no good, Mrs. Barker will have to find another Mrs. Prior. And then we won't have to tell our Mums about it at all. I felt better then. I could think this all out for myself. And I knew Sadie would be on my side.

I heard Sadie ask about her big sister. So I asked about

my cousin Theresa, and my Uncle Yudi, and of course about my Dad. Was everybody all right? But if things were quiet, why wouldn't everybody be all right?

We spent the rest of the time walking around the town. Part of me was really angry at my Mum saying all the time how lucky I was. And another part of me was sorry I was angry.

They wanted to go back to London before the blackout. So we took them to the station. How I wanted to get on that train too and go back to the muck of Stepney, to my old unshiny house, without the nice garden, without the polished floors, and even with the toilet in the yard.

I didn't care if there were bombs or not. I suppose our Mums knew better and we would have to stay here forever—or at least until Christmas. I would start counting the days.

12

School Again

WHEN SCHOOL finally started what a muddle it was!

We had left the house in good time because we wanted to be early. Mrs. Barker had changed her mind and didn't make us polish floors that day, she said, as it was the first day of school. Just a little dusting, and the usual bed-making and washing up. But we would have to make up for it another day.

We saw many Stortford girls walking along the High Street on their way home. Some glared at us, others walked by with their noses in the air, and some even poked tongues at us. I wanted to stick my foot out and trip them. There was never a smile from that lot. Maybe they thought we were going to infect their school or something.

As we arrived early, we were able to meet the other girls before the bell rang. We talked our heads off, and pretended everything was wonderful in our billets.

When the bell rang we were ushered through a beautiful wood paneled entrance hall with a wide flight of wooden stairs that led to the Headmistress' office, so we were told. A huge brass chandelier hung from the high, high ceiling. Later on we were told this hall was only used for visitors. The only children who went up those stairs were sent for some kind of punishment.

From there we marched along a narrow corridor into the Assembly Hall, which also was used as the gym. So much light was flooding into the room through the large windows, which stretched almost to the ceiling, that we had to blink when we entered. Miss Harris led our class to its place. Dr. Hunt walked onto the platform and a hush came over the whole school. We all rose. She was tall and thin, with her red hair piled in a bun on the top of her head. Just like the buns in Mr. Barker's shop, I thought, and smiled to myself.

Dr. Hunt bent her head and began the Lord's Prayer:

"Our Father . . . ." Her rimless glasses began to slip down her nose. She didn't look like a doctor, not even like a professor. But we all liked her very much. I always said the words of the Lord's Prayer to myself until I came to the word Jesus, and then always tried to think of something else. But I never could.

The prayer was soon over, and we raised our heads. Dr. Hunt was smiling.

"All right, girls, sit down, sit down," she said. "Let's get on with the business of the day. There is a lot to do.

"First, let me say how proud I am of the way you have settled in with your foster parents. I've had no complaints, which shows how happy you must be. Stortford is a lovely market town full of interesting things for you to see and do. Keep up the good work, girls.

"Now, although we're away from London . . . and as your parents have told you London is very quiet right now . . . one never knows if there might be an air raid here. So, for the first few days we're going to have air raid practice, just like fire drill. But if you're in the street and you hear a siren, go straight to an air raid shelter. They're clearly marked. And make very sure you're in your billets well before blackout time. That means you must go straight home from school. If you have any questions about air raid warnings, your form teacher will help you. Now I know there are some girls who are kosher, and so we are having a kosher community kitchen in the town. Food will be sent from London and those girls who only eat kosher will have a full hot lunch there before coming to school. Tickets will be fourpence and the office will provide them."

I squeezed Sadie's hand. "Thank goodness," I whispered. I felt as if a great burden had been taken away from me.

Then Dr. Hunt directed the teachers to take us to our classrooms. Ours was on the second floor, and what a mess it was. Those Stortford girls really didn't want us there. The rows of desks were all crooked, the inkwells almost empty, and the desks were locked, so we would have to keep our books in our satchels. Miss Harris wasn't very pleased about this.

We straightened the rows, cleaned and filled the inkwells, and took our seats.

"I'm sorry you found this room in such a mess," Miss Harris said. "But we'll leave it just as we would like to find it, clean and tidy and everything in order. We won't allow them to have any complaints. Pity about the locked desks. But that can't be helped."

For the first few days we were very careful. And school went on its usual pattern, much the same as in London.

There was a netball court behind this school the same as we had in London. But then, behind that, we saw tennis courts.

"Oh, Sadie," I said. "How posh! Do you think they'll teach us to play?"

"I hope so," she said, and threw her arms around me. "Oh Kitty, how posh we're getting. But if only we lived

58

somewhere else, and not with the Barkers."

The weeks passed, and Christmas was drawing near. Our parents were not allowed to come down to see us until the holidays. We were so unhappy about this that I finally decided to write and tell my Mum about the charring. I had written and told her about the kosher food, about the soup and salami, the lovely mashed potatoes, and the treacle tart or suet pudding for sweet. But now I wrote to tell her why I wanted to come home:

> It's getting so cold now, Mummy, and our fingers
> are freezing when we're polishing the floors. And
> our knees are all scratched. We even have to polish
> all her brass, and the smell of the polish gets all up
> my nose. I hate it. We have to get up so early to get
> everything done before we go for lunch. I so want to
> come home. And Sadie feels the same.

One Saturday morning, while Sadie and I were on our knees polishing the front room, there was a knock at the door. Mrs. Barker went to open it and I heard, "Hello, Mrs. Simmonds." My heart did a somersault. What had happened? Why was Mummy here? I jumped up, nearly tripping over the apron I was wearing and raced to the door, throwing my arms around her.

She looked at me. Tears were welling up in her eyes.

"Kitty, what's happening? Why are your fingers so cold? And you look so dirty!" She must have realized then that what I had written was the truth. Mrs. Barker was watching us.

"Come. Have a cup of tea, Mrs. Simmonds, and I'll explain what's been happening."

She led us into the kitchen and began to make tea. I went back to call in Sadie.

"You see, my char fell and hurt herself, and the girls are helping out until I can find someone else. They don't work very hard, and I felt you wouldn't mind if they did this."

My mother scowled. "How can you take advantage of children, Mrs. Barker?" she said. "Haven't you ever had any of your own? Perhaps I'd better speak to Dr. Hunt!"

"Oh, please, don't do that, Mrs. Simmonds. If you feel so badly about this, I'll get somebody and won't let the girls do it any more. But please, don't go to the school. The girls are very happy here. It would be such a shame to send them somewhere else."

I didn't want to go somewhere else. I wanted to go home. But I knew my Mum. I knew she was scared of the bombs. And I knew that she wouldn't take me home if she thought something was going to happen in London.

Then I saw Sadie out of the corner of my eye standing in the doorway, her black hair all over her face.

"Sadie," my Mum said. "Do you like it here?"

Sadie shrugged her shoulders and didn't answer. She was a bit scared of Mrs. B.

"I came down on the spur of the moment," my Mum said. "When I got your letter, Kitty, I didn't believe it. So, I took an excursion from Liverpool Street. I know that your parents can't leave the shop on Saturday, Sadie. So

I didn't even speak to them. Come here, luv." And she hugged Sadie.

"Kitty is going to come home for the school holiday if London's quiet," my Mum said. "Perhaps your Mum and Dad will let you come, too. I'll go 'round and ask them when I get home. But let's not have all this housework, Mrs. Barker! I'm ever so grateful that you're having the girls, but it's hard enough for them to be away from home without making it harder."

I looked at Mrs. Barker. She looked very glum. "Let's have a cup of tea," she said. "Maybe we'll all feel better."

We all sat down around the table. I looked at my Mum. I couldn't believe she was here. And I couldn't believe how she had stuck up for us. And I couldn't believe it was all my doing.

"I can only stay a little while, as I came on the excursion," she said. "I'd like the girls to walk back with me to the station. Perhaps we'll have a little treat on the way. But finish what you're doing first, girls, and then we'll all turn over a new leaf."

Maybe so. But thinking about going home for Christmas, even if Mrs. Barker didn't keep her word, made me feel so excited. I would soon be back in London, and maybe, maybe, I would never have to come back again.

13

Coming Home

THE WEATHER HAD BECOME much colder and the leaves had fallen from the trees. There was tons of rain. When it rained a lot at home all the walls in our house were wet, especially in my bedroom. But in this house, even with the pouring rain and the dark days, everything was dry as well as shiny.

Mrs. Barker didn't get another Mrs. Prior as she had promised. She told us that labour was hard to find because everyone was working in defence. We wondered why she didn't clean the house herself. She's too high and mighty for that, I supposed.

We continued to do our housework in the morning, lunching at the kosher kitchen, going to school in the afternoon, and willing the holidays to come quickly. After school, and after tea when the washing up was done, we did our homework, and once a week we wrote to our parents. My Dad was still away so I wrote to him, too. Then we would listen to the children's hour on the wireless. But mostly we wanted to hear what was happening in the war, and especially in London.

By the middle of December, it was still quiet there. And soon we would go. Our Mums had been sending us spending money. We now had more than the two shillings and a penny which was half fare one way. But the booking clerk at the station told us that it would be cheaper if we got a return ticket, as we were coming back.

We couldn't sleep the night before we were leaving. We lay awake listening to the rain pit pattering on the window pane and on the roof. I would wear the new Mac and Wellingtons my Mum had sent me.

I must have fallen asleep because the next thing I knew Sadie was shaking me. Opening my eyes, I saw the sun streaming through the window. It was already half past seven. I had overslept. We had planned to get up before dawn, even before we heard the rooster.

"I couldn't wake you," Sadie said. "You were talking in your sleep, and waving your arms. Do you remember?"

"Yes. I remember," I said. "I was trying to get out of our broken house. It was bombed, and everything was in my way. Do you think London is all right, Sadie?"

"Stop it," she said. "You're the one who wants to go home. And now I think you're scared."

"Honest, I'm not," I said. "I just don't want anything to happen to stop us."

"So let's go," she said. "Even if it's sunny, we should still put on Wellingtons. There must be lots of puddles from all that rain last night. Hurry up, Kitty. The Barkers are waiting to have breakfast with us as it's Sunday. And we don't want to miss the train."

"I wish we could have gone yesterday," I said. "But of course she had to make us work all day to make up for us being away."

"Oh, hurry up, Kitty, and stop talking." She grabbed my hand and we ran downstairs.

"My goodness," Mr. Barker said as we sat down.

"You're up bright and early for a Sunday morning. And you both look real chippa."

"We're going home for the holidays," I said. "Didn't Mrs. Barker tell you?"

"Gladys," he said, "we'll really miss these two, won't we? Now mind you come back as soon as you can. This place won't be the same without you."

I bet it won't, I thought.

We had packed the night before. I had wanted to take everything home, but I knew my Mum would be wild with me if I did. We seemed to have so much more than we had originally brought. But of course our Mums had sent us new clothes. Anyway, everything was ready, and if all was well we would stay home for two whole weeks.

The Barkers stood at the door and waved goodbye. We hurried to the station. Even though the sun was out, there were still lots of puddles in the street. We were glad we were wearing our Wellingtons.

We were early for the train. But there were a few other girls from school waiting, too. One girl said she was going home for good, and I envied her. The others were coming back just like us. Edie Finegold told us she was only going home for a while and then going by boat to America, to New York, to stay with her aunt until the war was over. What a long way to go just to be safe, I thought. And what a long time not to see your Mum. Some people said the war could go on for years. Not like the Hundred Years' War, I hoped.

After what seemed like the longest wait of my life, the train huffed and puffed into the station. We jumped into a compartment as soon as it stopped. It didn't wait long either. It knew perfectly well we wanted to get home.

We couldn't see out the window for a little while as the engine was belching so much steam. But finally it cleared and we saw the bare countryside flashing past. We were on our way home at last, even it was only for a visit.

We didn't talk. We just stared out the window waiting for the junction where the tracks would begin to crisscross. We would know we were getting nearer London because other trains would be coming from other places.

Then the countryside began to fall away, fewer fields and more houses, little houses with sooty roofs, and a few trees bare of leaves.

The rain had started again. The sky and the houses seemed blanketed in the same sooty grey.

More junctions. And then we were under Blackfriars Bridge.

Nearly there, I thought. My heart was racing.

Lots of shuttling, hissing. Lots of train tracks. And then, finally, there we were coming into the station. The train lurched to a stop, nearly knocking us off our seats. We were just outside the station waiting for our turn to pull in.

More jerks, and then a long pause. It seemed deathly silent on the train, as if everyone was holding his breath.

The lights flickered on and off. Then one final jerk and the train wheezed up to the platform.

Liverpool Street Station at last. I couldn't believe we were here. We picked up our cases and pulled open the door of the compartment the second it stopped. We hadn't told our Mums what train we were catching, so we didn't expect them to be at the barrier.

The platform was so wide. Smuts of soot were floating everywhere. Everyone was in a hurry. We hurried, too. I know I had seen the ticket collector before, but I didn't stop to think where. We gave him our ticket half and rushed through.

And there they were. Our Mums were waiting for us. They must have been sure we would get the first train out of Bishop Stortford that Sunday morning. There was a lot of hugging and kissing and then someone finally said, "Let's go home."

The station was a hustle and bustle of people. Instead of the porters I used to see pushing wagons and carrying cases, there were lots and lots of soldiers carrying their duffle bags or haversacks over their shoulders. There were airmen and sailors, too, waiting for their trains to take them to the war.

My Mum wanted to get us out of the station as quickly as she could. We went up the stairs and over the bridge to the entrance at Bishopsgate. The sun was streaming in. We could walk home from Liverpool Street. But Sadie and her Mum had to get the No. 6 bus to Hackney Road, where she lived, and where her Dad had his tailor's shop.

We decided to walk with them to the stop and wait with them till the bus came.

Everything seemed just the same as when I had left. People were still rushing around. There was still litter on the streets. The paper man was still selling his papers outside the station. Dirty Dicks, the pub across the road from the bus stop, still looked the same.

Perhaps I had dreamt it. Perhaps there wasn't a war on after all.

When Sadie's bus came, my Mum and I crossed over to Middlesex Street for the fifteen-minute walk home.

"Why are you looking around all the time, Kitty?" my Mum asked.

I had been twisting my neck looking for changes. But there weren't any that I could see.

"I can't believe I'm home, Mum, and that nothing has changed."

"Oh, yes, it has," she said. "You'll see lots of windows boarded up in case of broken glass. And every night we have to use blackout curtains, the same as you do in Bishop Stortford."

"But everything still looks the same to me."

As it was Sunday morning, there were lots of people going to Petticoat Lane which was just nearby.

"We'll go down the Lane later," my Mum said. "I put a deposit on a nice little dress for you and I want to put another shilling on it before someone else grabs it."

"Let's go now, Mum," I said. "It's on the way home."

"All right. But we can't be long. Uncle Yudi's dying

to see you. He's probably got some joke up his sleeve for you. We'll go straight to the shop. I don't want that dress to go."

Petticoat Lane was crowded as usual. It was almost lunchtime, so some of the stalls were starting to pack it in. By one o'clock on Sundays the Lane closed.

But there was everyone as before. The pickle lady was still at the corner of Casson Street behind her barrels of salt herrings and pickles. Her white apron still had finger marks all over it. And she was still yelling her wares. Whenever someone asked for one, down would go her head almost into the barrel, and out would come a lovely big golden herring soaked in brine. Her fingers were red as beets from the cold and from wiping them dry on her apron. Today my Mum bought from her, too.

Then there was Barnet's, the butcher, with links of sausages hanging from great big hooks on the ceiling. They looked like pink paper chains that we used to decorate our house for Chanukah. And there was the great big pot of sizzling water cooking saveloys, fat and plump and brown, the steam rising right up to the ceiling. Their smell made me so hungry. The place was crowded as usual with people eating those hot saveloys and salt beef sandwiches, treading in the thick sawdust on the floor.

Then there were the dress shops with so many dresses hanging on hangers outside, the men yelling at you to come and try one on. They looked a lot older than I remembered, though. They must have been the Dads of the men who were there before. I suppose their sons were soldiers now.

"Mummy," I said. "Look! The cat's meat man. He's still there. Have we still got Tibby, Mum?"

"Yes. But you know we don't buy that meat even for the cat. Come, let's hurry on."

We pushed our way through to the children's shop. My Mum paid another shilling deposit, and said I'd have the dress before I went back to school. It was navy velvet with a white collar and ever so nice. My Mum really knew what I liked and what suited me. Everybody said so. Even when my Dad was out of work before the war my Mum always dressed me nicely, everybody said. I gave my Mum a big hug. And then we hurried home, down Brick Lane to our street.

My little Uncle Yudi was waiting in the doorway of the shop, his cap on the side of his head and a lighted Woodbine in the corner of his mouth.

"Allo, Kit. It ain't 'alf nice to see you." He gave me a big hug, his Woodbine still in his mouth. "You're just in time to do me a big favour. Run round the corner, will ya, and get me a pound of rubber nails?"

I was just about to run back up the street when Uncle Yudi let out a laugh.

"Rubber nails?" I asked. "Oh, Uncle Yudi! Not again!" He gave me a big wink.

"Leave her alone, Yudi," my Mum said. And we all laughed.

How wonderful it was to be home again.

14

Home at Last

WE WENT THROUGH the shop into the house. My Uncle Yudi ran a milk shop and we lived behind it and above it. He sold butter and cream and, of course, milk which was served from large metal churns using half-pint and pint metal measures which hung on the side of the churns.

The entrance to our house was really at the side of the shop, but we never went that way if the shop was open.

Sometimes my uncle just closed the shop whenever he felt like it. He'd put the great wooden shutters across the large front window, hold them in place with a long black iron bar and then go off to a bookie to bet on the horses. That's when my mother would get really angry with him.

"You'll lose all your money again, Yudi, and you haven't got much anyway. And I haven't time to look after your shop, the few shillings it brings in."

"Oh, Passie," he would say. "Just shut the shop, and bugga' the customers." And he'd be off with a twinkle in his eye, a great big grin, and a cigarette dangling from the corner his mouth.

We all went into the kitchen. Uncle Yudi had the kettle on already.

"All right, luv," he said as he went to the cupboard. "'Ere's my favourite, currant cake from Sainsbury's. You don't get this in the country, I'm sure."

We sat down and he cut us each a thick slice. It was good. And as usual, Uncle Yudi began to pick the currants out of his cake.

"I thought you love this cake, Uncle Yudi," I said.

"You remember, girl," he said. "I love the cake. I love the cherries. But I 'ate the currants. So I pick 'em out."

"Oh, uncle," I said, "you are funny." And he gave my cheek a great big pinch.

"Oooouch!" I shrieked.

There was a fire burning in our Blacklead stove. Uncle Yudi must have gone out and got some Blacklead and put it on to make it look good just for me. My Mum usually did that every Friday for the Sabbath. But this time he must have wanted to make it look especially good for me.

Even the mantelpiece above it was clear. And the brass pestle was empty of his cigarette stubs. But a few betting slips were still stuck in the corner of the big gilt mirror over the mantelpiece.

"They're for a big race at the end of the week, girl," he whispered. "I don't want to lose 'em."

How my Mum and Dad hated him playing the horses! He'd win one day and lose it all the next. He never had any money.

"Why don't you lie down for a bit on the sofa," my Mum said. "You must be tired." She put a cushion behind me.

"I'm not ill, Mum," I said. "Why are you making all this fuss?"

"You look so done in!" she said. "We'll have something to eat, and then you can go upstairs and have a rest."

"Mummy," I said, "I don't want to have a rest. I want to see everything."

I looked around. There was the little hole at the end of the sofa, with the straw trying to come out, and the patch over it which would never stick on properly. There was the little wireless on the mantelpiece that Auntie Ray had given us. And the big kitchen table was covered with a white oilcloth.

"Mum, you've moved the furniture around again," I said. "Before I left the table was against the other wall facing the yard and the sofa was by the table."

"I know," she said. "But it makes more room this way. And the sofa is closer to the fire. It's cold now, and coal is soon going to be rationed, and we must save. The coalman doesn't come as often as he used to. His boy has gone into the army, you know."

I used to love to watch that coalman, with the great big sacks of coal on his cart. He would heave a sack onto his back and walk down our passage, dropping bits as he went, and piling it with a clobber and a tumble into the coal cupboard under the stairs. Sometimes I didn't know how he got out of that coal cupboard, because he'd have to climb right into it to empty the sacks. His face was always so black. When he left, we had to sweep the whole passage because of the bits of coal he had dropped. My Mum also used the coal to make the fire under the boiler in the yard when she did her washing.

"I don't want to have a rest, Mum," I said. "I want to see the rest of the house. Is Mrs. Reingold still here?" She was our lodger, who rented a room on the first floor. A nice old lady.

"She's not well, Kitty. So don't bang your feet when you go upstairs. I'll skin this herring and we'll have it with some cheese and black bread when you come down. And tonight we'll have your favourite supper."

"Toad in the Hole, Mum?"

She nodded her head. How lucky could I be?

I clomped up the stairs. How many times had I slid down those lino covered stairs, I thought, as I passed Mrs. Reingold's room? I didn't want to see her today. She was always complaining, always acting as if she was going to die at any moment. I went straight into the front room, where my cousin Theresa slept on a Put-u-up bed in the corner. The rest of the room was our parlour. There was a gramaphone and my piano. Two brass candle holders were attached to the front panels of the piano. And on top of the piano there was a glass case containing a bride and groom made of sugar. They were standing on the top layer of my Mum and Dad's wedding cake. It was still there.

I sat down at the piano and tried to play Chopsticks. I still remembered how to play it and that was good. A green chenille tablecloth covered the round table in the middle of the room. The big green flower bowl my Auntie Leah had given us still sat in the middle of the table. I think Theresa used that pot for other things besides flowers. At least that's what my Dad once told me.

I went up another flight of stairs, past the sink on the next landing, past my Uncle Yudi's room, to the large front bedroom which I shared with my Mum and Dad. Their big bed was by the door, and my single bed was in a corner by the window. My Dad had made all the furniture himself, including the huge wardrobe against one wall.

I unpacked my things and put them in the wardrobe and lay down on my bed. The blinds were half down and the sun was trying to peek through. I got up and looked out the window. The flats opposite were so close I felt that I could put out my hand and touch their grey walls. There was no green and no grass. But it was home and I was happy.

I heard Tibby meowing. She jumped on my bed, and I shushed her off. I liked Tibby but not to cuddle or get too close to. I remembered now that my Mum had helped her when her kittens were born. Tibby had climbed up the ladder outside our bedroom to have her kittens in the loft. My Mum had to climb up after her and get her down. We kept those kittens for a long time, until someone around the corner wanted them and we gave them away.

"Kitty," my Mum called up the stairs. "Come down and have something to eat."

"Coming!"

I slowly went downstairs and straight out into the yard to go to the lavatory, and then to the kitchen to wash my hands. And then we all sat down to herring and black bread, and Uncle Yudi's homemade cream cheese, made in a little white cotton sack especially for me.

Tomorrow I would help in the shop and make cheese, too. And if Uncle Yudi had to run to play the horses, I would serve the customers instead.

What a lovely day this had been!

15

Holidaying At Home

I LOVED BEING HOME, even with the shabbiness. No polished floors. No carpets. And dustballs all over the place.

The house was crowded. My Dad was still away, but Theresa and Uncle Yudi were there. Mrs. Reingold was upstairs, her grown-up children coming to see her all the time. Theresa was working in a factory but had a boyfriend who came around evenings. He was soon going into the air force, or so he said. Sometimes I would see them cuddling in the passage before he went home. My Mum liked him. She said he was a clean living boy. I didn't know what that meant, but his face was always bright and he looked clean to me.

My uncle made a fuss of me and let me serve in the shop. I suppose it was good for him. With me around he could run to play the horses more often and wouldn't have to close the shop as he did before. He was also in the Air Raid Precautions—or the ARP as we called it. Wearing a white armband, he would go on his rounds after dark checking to see if any blackout curtains had not been drawn. If there were any chinks of light, he would call up: "Bloody Jerry'll 'it you if you don't close that curtain, mate!" I think people must have been scared of him, even though he was very short. When he wasn't checking curtains, he went on firewatch patrol. Even though there hadn't been any air raids yet, everyone had to be on the alert.

There were few children around. All the children from my street were still away so there was nobody to play with. Sadie lived quite a way from me and as we didn't have a phone I said I would go round to see her with my Mum before we went back.

Meanwhile I helped in the shop, which was not very busy. I loved to pat and weigh the butter, putting a blob of the yellow butter on greaseproof paper using ridged pats to make a square, and trying to cut the exact weight the customer asked for. People usually bought just a quarter pound, or even two ounces. But I managed. Milk was delivered in metal churns. I would reach into the churn holding the measure and pour the milk into a glass bottle, and put the cardboard cap on carefully so that it wouldn't tip into the bottle and spill milk all over me. The churn was so high I had to stand on a stool to do this and was often scared I would tip over into the churn myself. But sometimes people came in with their own jugs and then it was easier.

The shop was closed on Saturday for the Sabbath. On Friday afternoon Uncle Yudi would close up the shutters. My Mum would scrub the shop, the kitchen floor and the passage. Then she'd make a half circle of hearthstone chalk around the front door, making the pavement all white and clean. Every other Jewish house on the street did the same.

Although the shop was closed the door was left open, so that when we came home in the evening we had to push open that brown heavy shop door and feel our way though the darkened shop to the kitchen. It was eerie . . . but comfortable, too.

The first week passed by very quickly. On Monday, New Year's Eve, the postman brought a letter and a Christmas card from the Barkers. My Mum thought it was very nice of them to send it. But when she read the letter she began to cry.

"What is it, Mum," I asked. "Has somebody died?"

"Oh, no, Kitty," she said, "but Mrs. Barker has signed the letter 'From Your Foster Mother.' You'll have no foster mother, Kitty! I'm your mother and always will be. Remember that!"

"What's a 'foster mother?'" I asked.

"It means that if anything happens to me, Kitty," she mumbled, "she'll have to be your Mum."

"No she won't, you know!" I said.

She started to cry again.

"I'm sorry, Kitty. But since your Dad has been away my nerves have been so bad."

"Mum, let's go round to Sadie and see if she got the letter too," I said.

She dried her eyes, hugged me, and put on the kettle for tea. She always did that when she was in a state.

Uncle Yudi was home so we didn't have to shut the shop to go. There was no direct bus to take us to Sadie's so it was quicker to walk. We never thought of taking buses short distances anyway.

Sadie lived in Goldsmith's Row, not very far from Hackney Hospital. It was a long narrow street with shops on either side. Before I knew Sadie my Mum used to take me to the Dolls' Hospital there when one of my dolls got broken. They would fix on a new arm or leg, or patch up a face that someone had trod on. So I knew the street. Sadie's father had a tailor shop and they lived in the house behind it. We knew they would be home because it wasn't Sunday, or Christmas or Boxing Day when all the shops had to close.

We found the shop. It was small and dark. Mr. Davidovitch was huddled over the sewing machine, his nose almost touching the needle, his foot tread-treadling away. Mrs. Davidovitch was sitting near him felling the bottom of a pair of trousers. I knew it was felling because my Mum used to bring work home from a factory and fell hems to earn a little extra money when my Dad was out of work. There was a large pressing board nearby, too, and huge heavy irons on a gas ring behind. I could smell the steam from the wet cloths he used to press the clothes.

Mrs. Davidovitch looked up. When she saw us, a big smile came over her face.

"Hello, Mrs. Simmonds," she said. "What a nice surprise! Oh, Kitty, there you are, dear! How are you enjoying the holidays? Sadie will be so glad to see you. She's downstairs in the kitchen."

The kitchen was in the basement below the shop. Behind this shop was a storeroom for the cloth. And upstairs was their parlour and bedrooms, Sadie showed me later.

Mrs. Davidovitch put down her felling and led the way downstairs. Sadie was there alone, playing. She was so glad to see me. Mr. D., of course, didn't come down. He had to mind the shop and do his work. But he said he would see us later.

"Oh, Kitty," Sadie said, "I've been so lonely here all by myself. Nobody to play with. And you live so far away. I wouldn't even care if I went back to the Barkers now."

"Sadie, I've been busy in the shop helping Uncle Yudi. I don't want to go back there. But if you go back, I suppose I'll have to go too."

My Mum and Mrs. D. were talking and I heard the word 'foster mother', and then "I'll give her!" My Mum looked really angry.

"It's nothing, Mrs. Simmonds," Mrs. D. said. "It's just what they call themselves. It doesn't mean anything. Don't worry about it.

"Anyway, they have to go back. There's so much talk on the wireless now about air raids. They say Hitler is walking all over Europe. The raids here could start any day now.

"Now, now, don't cry, Mrs. Simmonds. Nothing's going to happen to them . . . or us. And even if it did, you've got sisters who'd look after Kitty."

This made my Mum start crying even harder. "If I keep her here," she sobbed, "she may get killed by a bomb. Sooner me than her!"

On and on it went, until Mrs. D. put the kettle on for tea and we all calmed down. Our Mums decided that we would go back the following Sunday, but made us promise that we would never, but never, call the Barkers "foster parents."

We had a lovely afternoon and arranged that Sadie's Mum would bring Sadie round on Thursday afternoon and she could help me in the shop.

That night my Mum and I lay in bed together. Before the war I used to love New Year's Eve. The church at the end of the street would peel out the old year. We would hear people coming home from pubs or parties singing away. But this year no church bells were allowed because of the war. But we still heard people on their way home singing *Oh, Jerusalem,* or some people really drunk singing *Knock 'Em in the Old Kent Road.*

I snuggled up to my Mum in her big bed. Only a few days more before we have to go back to hard labour again, I thought. But I said, "I'll miss you Mum. Can I come back again soon, if it's still quiet in London?"

"For Pesach you'll come home," she said. But

Pesach—the Jewish festival of Passover—wasn't until spring, and that was such a long time away. I didn't want to argue and make my Mum miserable and cry again. And it was something to look forward to, I supposed.

"Oh, all right," I said. "I'll wish Pesach to come quickly."

How strange it was. Now that I was home, far from the Barkers, being there didn't seem so terrible. Maybe when I got back, it might not be as bad as before.

16

Noises in the Night

OUR MUMS DECIDED that we would all meet by the ticket barrier at the station that following Sunday morning.

I was sure I wouldn't sleep Saturday night. I wanted to stay up as late as my Mum would let me. In the afternoon, we had gone to see my aunties, Ray and Sarah, who lived quite a bus ride away. They were so glad to see me and gave me sixpence each.

"It's for sweets, Kitty," Auntie Ray said. "Buy something really sticky."

"Ray!" my Mum exclaimed. "She'll get bad teeth and pimples from eating sweets, you know." But she let me take the money all the same. It was nice to have two silver sixpences in my pocket.

By the time we caught the trolley bus home it was

almost dark, blackout time. We had our torches ready, just in case. It was a long walk from the bus to our house. Rain had made the streets slippery. We had to tread carefully through the rubbish of the market. Our street was narrow and dark. I gave a sigh of relief when we got to our door.

I lay in bed listening to my mother's heavy breathing in her big double bed at the other end of the room, and thinking about my Dad who couldn't come home for the holidays. He'd made everything in this room and was so proud of it. He even used to sole and heel our shoes, his iron last poking out from underneath my Mum's bed. I wanted so much to see him.

I heard my cousin Theresa come in and some noises in the passage. I suppose her boyfriend was there kissing her again. Then the door slammed. I hoped they hadn't had a row. Theresa came clumping up the stairs to her room on the first floor. Silence again, except for my Mum's heavy breathing. Then I heard Uncle Yudi come in. He crept up those stairs. I could hardly hear him. My Mum always said he was as light as a jockey. Still more heavy breathing. But I was as wide awake as ever.

Then I heard Theresa open her bedroom door and go downstairs. "Where is that bloody cat?" I heard her say. It was her job to give the cat some milk before she went to bed. Perhaps she'd had a row with her boyfriend and forgotten all about it. She was downstairs a long time, and then I heard her clumping back up again, swearing under her breath. I suddenly thought I heard meowing, but it wasn't coming from downstairs.

I crept out of bed. "Theresa," I whispered down. "I can hear meowing, and it's coming from up here."

"What's she doing up there?" Theresa whispered back. When she got to my landing we looked around in our room. No cat. We wouldn't go into Uncle Yudi's room. We hated to go in there. It always had such a funny smell.

Then Theresa said, "I think the meowing is coming from up in the attic." We listened, and yes it was.

There was a ladder flattened against the wall going from the landing outside our room up to the attic. As far as I knew there was nothing up there but a few trunks. I'd never been there myself.

"I'm going to climb up and see what's going on," Theresa whispered.

"Theresa, you can't," I hissed. "Mummy will kill you. She's the only one who knows how to get that ladder off the wall. It's hooked on to something or other."

"Then we'll have to wake her up!"

My Mum, who always said she was a light sleeper, was still snoring away.

"You wake her up, Theresa," I whispered. "She won't like it if I do. I'm going away again tomorrow, and I don't want her to be angry with me before I go."

Theresa crept up to my Mum's bed.

"Auntie Passie," she whispered. "Auntie Passie."

No answer, but less snoring.

"Auntie Passie. Auntie Passie."

She gently shook my Mum, who gave a jolt. She shook her head, trying to open her eyes.

"What's the matter? Www . . . what's the matter? Kitty, are you all right?

"It's Theresa, Auntie Passie. I think the cat's up in the attic. I wanted to climb up but Kitty won't let me. She said you're the only one who knows how. I bet the cat's up there having kittens, Auntie Passie."

"Oh my God, not again. She did it once before. How does she get up there? I don't believe this. In the middle of the night! Couldn't she have waited till morning?"

She rubbed her eyes, got out of bed, and put on her slippers.

"I'll fix the ladder and then go up and see what's going on. You stay down, Theresa. Hold the ladder and hold Kitty. I don't want her climbing up there."

Not a sound came from Uncle Yudi's room.

My Mum took the ladder from the wall and hooked it into place. She made sure it was firm and that Theresa was holding it and then slowly climbed up, her nightgown trailing behind her.

"Be careful, Mummy, be careful," I worried out loud. "You don't know what's up there."

"I know what's up there, Kitty. I know." She slowly disappeared into the hole. Now we could hear a great deal of meowing.

"Theresa, Kitty," Mummy called down. "You should see. She is having kittens. We have to help her." I didn't know anybody had to help a cat have kittens. But my

Mum stayed there quite a long time.

"I want to bring them down but Tibby won't let me," Mummy called down finally. "Kitty, run downstairs. Under the counter in the shop is a box where we keep the eggs. Take them out and bring me the box with some straw in it. We must make her comfortable."

I ran downstairs, found the box, made sure there weren't any eggs in it, and ran up again. My Mum was just saying to Theresa, "We'll make them comfortable and bring them down later. Now Kitty, as Theresa is holding the ladder, run down again and bring up a nice saucer of milk for Tibby."

I ran down again, found the enamel saucer the cat drank from, poured some milk in it, and carefully brought it upstairs. My Mum took up the box and then the milk. When she came down, she sat on the bottom rung of the ladder.

"What a night!" she said. "I think we'd better all go back to bed. Tomorrow's going to be a busy day."

But when I was in bed again, I still couldn't sleep. Would Bishop Stortford be as exciting as this? How could it be? But I'd make the best of it. And if it wasn't good, I'd find a way to change it. Soon it would be Pesach and I'd come home to a houseful of kittens, if my Mum hadn't given them away. Thinking about it all, I finally fell asleep.

Morning came quickly. We had to hurry to get to the train on time. Even old Mrs. Reingold came down to say goodbye and gave me a threepenny bit for spending money. Theresa, who always slept late, especially Sunday morning, was up early. She wanted to come to the station.

My Mum had packed my things the day before. She had given me extra stuff, including the new dress she had bought for me in Petticoat Lane plus lots of sweets and a homemade cake. She said she wanted to send something back for Mrs. Barker but I told her I wouldn't take it even if she bought it. But I promised I would share my sweets and cake.

Sadie and her Mum were already there when we arrived, just as the porter was blowing his whistle. We ran for the train, our Mums dragging our cases behind them. I was glad we were late. I didn't want to go through a long round of goodbyes.

The porter threw our bags into a compartment. The train gave a big jolt, huffed, puffed, and pulled out with lots of hissing. We leaned out of the window and waved and threw kisses. Then we sank miserably into corner seats.

17

A New Beginning

THE TRAIN WAS CROWDED with soldiers. They didn't take much notice of two girls in brown school uniforms huddled in the corner of a compartment. Maybe they were too busy thinking of people they had left behind, just as we were.

The train stopped at every little station on the way. Porters didn't call out the names of the stations now. We had to be on the alert so as not to miss ours. All too soon the name Bishop Stortford loomed up.

Nobody was at the station to meet us, although we had written and told the Barkers when we were coming. We dragged our cases back to their house, hoping at least that someone would be in when we arrived. They were in, and seemed glad to see us. Mr. Barker gave us a great big smile, and chuckled, and even Mrs. B. put an arm around our shoulders as if she really was happy to see us.

Perhaps things had changed.

We had tea and went to our room, which was exactly as we had left it. Yet the house didn't look as shiny as before. I blinked. Did I really see dust on the hall table as we went upstairs?

But things hadn't changed after all. Life went on as before. We still had to do our charring in the morning. We went to school in the afternoon, talked to our friends about our billet, complained, but never told the teachers.

January and February were very cold and the Barkers' house was not well heated. Because of the war there was a shortage of coal. It wasn't really rationed, but everyone was asked to go easy, so the Barkers only made a fire on Sundays at tea time. Our fingers would get numb, especially when we polished the floor. They would become quite white, and we would have to put them into our mouths to warm them up.

We looked forward to every word from home, and

when a parcel came we were so excited. There would be cake and biscuits and sweets. But Mrs. Barker said we couldn't keep food in our room, only in the larder.

"Anyway," she said, "sweets are bad for your teeth. I'll look after your parcels. I'm sure your Mums wouldn't want you to have them all at once. And rationing will be coming soon. You'll be glad you saved them."

It was so unfair.

When we first came back, Pesach didn't seem too far away, but now, after just a few weeks, it seemed like it would never come. I so wanted to go back home.

One cold, wet February day, with the damp seeping through every floorboard in the house, I was sitting in our bedroom after supper. Sadie was there, too. I had finished my homework, what I could do of it, and began to write a song about Mrs. Barker. Sadie said I shouldn't. But I was so miserable, I just felt I had to do something.

It took a little while, especially with Sadie looking over my shoulder.

"Don't say that, Kitty," she kept on saying. "If she finds it, you'll really get into trouble."

"How will she find it?" I said. "I'll keep it in my satchel."

Finally I finished the song and sang it for Sadie:

When we go polishing her floor each day
Her fat face is a boom
We'll have to tell old Doctor Hunt
We can't do out her room.

She's such a blinkin' ol' cow you know
A stingy miser too
While we are doing all her work
She hasn't anything to do.
We don't grumble
When she grabs all our sweets
We, like big fools,
We give her our ration of meat.
And when we polish don't she realize
Our fingers are numb with cold
Of course she wouldn't understand
'Cause we are in her hold.

I burst into laughter and then Sadie did, too.

"I wish I had a ukulele, Sadie," I said. "It's a real George Formby song." We laughed and laughed so much. It was such a lark.

"Put it away and hide it," Sadie said. So I put it in the bottom of my satchel, where nobody would find it.

A few days later, during French class with Miss McNaughton who taught French with a Scottish accent, a prefect came into the classroom and whispered something in her ear. Miss McNaughton turned and looked straight at me.

"All right," she said, "as soon as I finish teaching this song."

At the end of class Miss McNaughton said, "Kitty, Dr. Hunt would like to speak to you. Right now."

I turned beet red. What was it? Had anything

happened to my Mum or my Dad, to Theresa or Uncle Yudi? Why would Dr. Hunt want me? I hadn't done anything wrong in school, as far as I knew. Why would she want me?

I raced up the stairs and stood outside her office, trembling. I knocked.

"Come in."

There she was, lovely Dr. Hunt, her hair still pinned on top of her head like the buns in Mr. Barker's shop. But today she was not smiling.

"Hello, Kitty," she said. "You'd better sit down."

"Has anything happened to my Mum or Dad or anyone in my family? Why do you want me?"

I had often been sent to Dr. Hunt before for talking in class or doing other things I shouldn't. But these past months I had been good. I wasn't talking too much. I hadn't been late for school. My schoolwork was all right. I was keeping up. Why would she want me?

"Kitty," she said, "Mrs. Barker was here this morning. She said she found something that you had written. Is this yours?" She handed me my song.

I looked at it and tears welled up in my eyes. "Yes, it's mine, Dr. Hunt," I said. "I wrote it."

"Mrs. Barker is very, very upset", she said. "She's a very fine lady. And she's been very good to you. How could you do such a thing? If you had any complaints you should have come to me. Sadie has been there with you and she hasn't complained. Can you explain this to me?"

I told Dr. Hunt what we had been doing for Mrs.

Barker. I told her that my mother had come and told Mrs. Barker that we were not to be scivvies.

But Dr. Hunt insisted, "You had no business to write such a song. You have no right to call Mrs. Barker names."

I was so upset! Why hadn't Mrs. Barker come to me first? Why had she gone straight to Dr. Hunt? And how did she find the song? Had it slipped out, or . . . .

"Now, you will go and apologize to Mrs. Baker," Dr. Hunt said. "And you will tell her how upset I am with you also. If we were in London now I would suspend you. But as we're evacuated, I just can't do that."

If we were in London, I thought, I wouldn't have needed to write that song.

She also gave me five hundred lines: I must respect my elders and not be rude to people who are kind to me. I was only to do the lines in playtime.

I was so angry. Not about the punishment. Who cared about not going out to play or about writing lines? But that horrible Mrs. Barker to have come to Dr. Hunt without even telling me first! That really made me wild. I felt the blood rush to my neck and up to my face. And then my eyes filled with tears.

"I don't think the punishment is so bad, Kitty," Dr. Hunt said. "You could have been expelled, you know."

"It's not that," I said. "But couldn't she have told me first?"

Dr. Hunt didn't say any more so I stood up and left the room.

When I got back to class, everyone was staring at me,

especially Sadie. I slid into my desk beside her.

"What did she say?" Sadie whispered.

"Tell you later," I said.

I couldn't concentrate on the class. It was Geography and I liked Miss Smith. She was young and pretty and I always did well in her class. Today she kept telling me to wake up and stop daydreaming. Little did she know!

I couldn't wait for school to be over that day. It was after playtime so I wouldn't have to do those lines until tomorrow.

But there wouldn't be a tomorrow. I would see to that.

18

An End of It

WHEN SCHOOL WAS OVER and class dismissed, the girls huddled round me.

"What did Dr. Hunt want?" they asked. "Is everything all right in London?"

I didn't want to speak to anybody. I just wanted to go back to the house and give Mrs. Barker a piece of my mind. I ran out of class with Sadie running behind.

"Wait, Kitty," she said, "I'm coming, too! What's up?"

Only when I reached our road and was quite out of breath did I stop and let Sadie catch up with me.

"Kitty," she said, "give over! Tell me what's up!"

"It's that song, Sadie," I said. "She found it and took it to Dr. Hunt, without even telling me first. She must have looked in my satchel. It couldn't have fallen out. And why would she look in my satchel anyway? Did she think I'd stolen something from her that she had to look in my satchel? She's a bloody old cow. I'm glad I wrote that song. I'm not going to stay in that house another day. How did she know it was mine and not yours? I didn't have my name on it."

Sadie didn't know what to say. She seldom answered back. She was a goody-goody. The Barkers knew that. Sadie knew I knew it, too. She went quite red.

"I'm ever so sorry you're in trouble Kitty," she said. What shall I do?"

"What you like," I said, and ran on ahead.

The door was open. I ran straight up to our room, Sadie following me. She washed her hands for tea, but I just lay on my bed. Mrs. Barker's voice came bawling up the stairs. "Come down for tea, girls."

"Not me," I said to Sadie. "I'll go without her lousy tea tonight. I'm going to talk to her later." Sadie tried to make me go down, but I wouldn't. Of course she went down. Good as always.

"Kitty! Will you come down, now!" Mrs. Barker's voice again.

"No, Mrs. Barker," I yelled down. "I'm not hungry for your food. I'll come down after." Then I heard her footsteps storming up the stairs and she was at the door of our room, her face as red as a beetroot.

"What do you mean by that, Kitty?"

"I mean, Mrs. Barker, that I don't want your tea. I hate you. Couldn't you have spoken to me about that song before you took it to my school? And how did you find it anyway?" And I burst into tears.

"You ungrateful child," she said. "Sadie wouldn't speak to me like that."

"Sadie has no guts," I said.

She slammed the door and went back downstairs.

This time I was determined not to stay another day. I would go home by myself and wouldn't tell anybody. I had my spending money, enough for a half fare to London. I would go in the morning, and nobody would know.

While Sadie was having her tea, I emptied my satchel, and put my school books in the drawer. Then, I put what clothes I could into the satchel, not forgetting the lovely dress my Mum had bought me in Petticoat Lane. I couldn't get much more in but I pushed in clean knickers and a clean vest against the cold.

When Sadie came upstairs, I pretended I was asleep. But she knew I wasn't and she came over to my bed.

"Kitty," she said. "What can I do to make you feel better?"

I started to cry again.

"I bet Mr. Barker doesn't know what happened today," Sadie said. "He's not home yet. But I bet he wouldn't've let her take that song to the school. I just know it."

"Maybe you're right," I sniffled. "But he's not here.

And she took the song. And I hate her. And she hates me. And she likes you! Wouldn't surprise me if she likes you because of all the presents your Mum and Dad give her."

"What a terrible thing to say, Kitty! I thought you were my friend."

"I know! But why does she like you better than me? That's the only reason I can think of."

Then Sadie started to cry.

"Oh Sadie," I said. "Why don't we both leave and go home?"

"We can't! Our Mums would kill us. And so would Dr. Hunt. I hate it here too, Kitty! But there's nothing we can do."

I thought of my plan, and stopped crying. I wouldn't say one word to her about it, though, in case she'd tell.

I think I fell asleep smiling.

The next morning when I went down to breakfast Sadie was already there. And Mr. Barker was, too. He was all smiles. Mrs. B., of course, wasn't smiling at all.

I said "Good Morning" to her, but not a word about yesterday. And, of course, I didn't apologize.

After breakfast Sadie and I did our housework. Then we got ready to go to the community kitchen for lunch, and on to school.

I picked up my satchel. It looked a little more bulky than usual, but nobody noticed. I told Sadie I had packed my Mac in case it rained coming home. She didn't think anything of it.

When we were about a street away from school, I told

Sadie I had forgotten my homework and had to go back to the house for it. I told her to go on without me or she'd be late. Sadie never liked to be late, and so she just went on her way.

"Thank goodness for that," I thought.

But I didn't go straight to the train station. Instead, I waited until I was sure everyone was in school. Then I doubled back the way I had come—for a little way anyway—and dawdled my way toward the station, clutching my satchel.

I wasn't sure how long I'd have to wait for the next train to London. But with my two-and-a-penny half-fare in my hand I went up to the booking office to buy my ticket.

"What time is the next train to London?" I asked.

"In half an hour, dear," the booking clerk said. "Are you travelling alone?"

"Oh, yes," I said. "My Mum sent me the money. My Dad's coming home on leave so I'm to go down to see him."

"Does your school know?" he asked.

"Oh, yes. Of course." I trembled. "My Mum sent a letter to my headmistress."

"That's all right then," he said. "But you be careful now! Girls shouldn't be going on trains by themselves. It's not far to London, though. I'm sure your Mum's meeting you at the other end!"

"Oh, yes," I lied.

I couldn't wait to get away from that booking clerk.

I didn't want to wait on the platform in case the porter would start asking questions, too, and then I would have to tell more lies.

This was terrible. I had never told lies. And now look what was happening to me!

I went to the Ladies' Room to wait until I heard the train, and felt safe in there.

It seemed forever until I heard the puff-puffing of the train coming into the station. It seemed like the wheels were clacking out: Kitty is running away. Clank, clank. Kitty is free. She's free.

When I heard the train stop, I tore out of the Ladies' Room clutching my satchel tightly. My heart racing, I pulled open a compartment door and jumped in. I still didn't feel quite safe. The porter could still come and drag me out, even now. I took off my school velour and slumped into a corner seat, trying not to let my frizzy hair show above the window.

Thank goodness the compartment was empty.

I wanted to lie down on the floor until the train left. But if anyone walking along the corridor saw me it would be worse. So I huddled in the corner, holding my breath, and prayed for the train to get started.

The station was quiet now except for a few doors slamming. And then, finally, the porter blew his whistle, and with some jerks, stops and starts the train finally left Bishop Stortford.

For me, I hoped it was forever.

When we cleared the station, and I began to see

meadows, I finally sat up. Two airmen and a WAAF were talking in the corridor. After a bit, they slid open my compartment door and sat down opposite me.

The WAAF looked straight at me.

"Hello!" she said. "What's a girl like you doing on a train all by herself?"

"Oh," I said. "I'm going home to see my Dad. He's coming on leave from the Army. I haven't seen him for ever such a long time."

"Is your Mum meeting you at the other end?"

"Of course," I said. "She's working in munitions. But she's getting time off, too."

More lies! Once I started it seemed I just couldn't stop.

"I don't live far from Liverpool Street," I said. "So even if she doesn't get off in time, I can walk home. She sent me the key. I really don't want to miss school. But I'm dying to see my Dad!"

"You be careful, then!" she said.

Just then the ticket inspector slid open the door of the compartment.

"Can I see your pass, luv," he said to the WAAF. The airmen showed their passes, too.

"And who's are you, little one?"

"Here's my ticket," I said. "I'm going to see my Dad. He's coming home on leave."

"Travelling by yourself, dear?"

"Yes!" I said, sitting up straight.

He raised his eyebrows, and looked at the WAAF who was talking to the two airmen.

"I can't understand parents these days," he said. "Letting children travel alone, in wartime."

He mumbled more to himself as he left the compartment. I sank back down into my seat. I could breathe again.

"Please hurry, Liverpool Street," I prayed. "I must get home."

Of course my Mum wasn't waiting at the barrier to meet me. I hadn't told her or anyone else I was coming.

I hurried through, up the stairs, over the bridge, and out the door marked Bishopsgate. I wanted to run. But I knew I didn't dare in case someone might ask where I was going or what was my hurry.

My heart in my mouth, I walked quickly through Middlesex Street to Petticoat Lane, my steps only slowing as I neared my street.

What would my Mum say when she saw me? Would she even be home?

Finally, I rounded the corner of our street and saw our shop. But before I could get to it, I saw Mrs. Greenberg, who lived in the buildings across the street, walking towards me. I didn't know whether she saw me. I ducked into the stable where I used to watch horses being shoed. I didn't want anyone to see me and start asking questions before I got to my Mum.

It seemed like everyone I knew was out. I suppose they were shopping. I saw Mrs. Reingold, our lodger, with a carrier bag, some fish sticking out of a newspaper, its eyes glaring at me.

Then I saw Theresa's Dad, my Uncle Davie, with his milk cart, the pint and half-pint bottles in wire baskets, and Uncle Davie calling out, "Milk, ladies!" He was wearing his striped blue-and-white apron and funny straw hat. Why did he have to come along just now?

I stayed in that stable a long time. There were no horses there now so it was a good hiding place. I waited until the street was empty and then ran the few yards to our shop. When I pushed open the door, the bell clinked.

Nobody came right away. I didn't want to go into the kitchen. I wanted to surprise my Mum. Finally, she opened the door into the shop and was just going behind the counter when she realized who it was standing there.

I think she nearly fainted.

"What are you doing here, Kitty? Is something wrong? Am I seeing things? You should be in the country. Am I asleep or am I having those terrible dreams again?"

"It's all right, Mum. It is me. I'm really here. Don't faint. I wanted to see you so much that I came home."

"Where's Sadie?" my Mum said. "Did she come with you?

"No, she stayed there. But I really wanted to see you and Uncle Yudi. I couldn't wait until Pesach so I came home."

She put her arms around me and we went into the kitchen. There was Uncle Yudi, holding a piece of toast on a fork in front of the fire. When he saw me, he nearly dropped the fork into the fire. The bread almost fell off.

"Well this is a nice surprise," he said. "Life's very quiet 'ere without you, girl. Your Mum and I 'aven't 'ad a row for a long time. But what ya doin' 'ere?"

"I wanted to see you, Uncle Yudi. So I came home."

"Does the school know you're home, Kitty?" my Mum asked. I wondered if they believed what I was saying. This time I couldn't lie.

"No, Mum. The school doesn't know. And neither does anyone else. But I'm not going back."

"Oh!" she yelled. "Are they going to worry! Oh, you're giving everybody trouble. I'm sure they'll call the police. Yudi, have you got some coppers? I must go and phone Mrs. Barker. Poor woman. She must be worried out of her wits."

Then Uncle Yudi joined in. "Your Mum's right, girl. And I don't usually stick up for 'er. You'll make everybody worry, girl. It isn't right. Take some coppers from the till, Passie, and go and phone Mrs. Barker, and tell her that Kitty's 'ere. Phone the 'eadmistress in the morning. I'll give 'er something to eat while you go phone, Passie. Quick, before they begin to worry."

My mother ran out. Then my uncle turned to me.

"Tell me girl, now tell me why you really came 'ome."

I didn't say anything.

"Was it something terrible girl? Did you steal something?"

"All right, Uncle, I'll tell you. But don't tell my Mum, even though she'll find out from Mrs. Barker. Or perhaps she won't have enough coppers to get the whole story."

I told him about the song, and a great big smile came over him.

"I never thought you'd do something like that, Kitty. You take after your Uncle Yudi, girl. I think that's a lark. Wait till your Mum finds out, though. She'll go mad. She always tried to bring you up like a real lady. Well, come and 'ave something to eat. And when she comes back she'll probably give you what for. That's if they told 'er why you came home. So you'd better go upstairs right after and I'll tell 'er you felt sick and went to sleep."

I was glad I told Uncle Yudi the truth. I knew he'd stick up for me when she would start on me tomorrow.

19

Battle Royal

MY MOTHER WAS UP bright and early the next morning. She pulled back the blackout curtains. It was a grey February day. I had been awake for a long time but pretended sleep, my head completely under the covers. She came over to my bed.

"All right, Kitty," she called, "time to get up, time to get up now! We'll have a nice breakfast and start off."

I pretended to be asleep. Mummy shook me.

"Kitty, I told Dr. Hunt that we'd come this morning."

Her voice grew tense. I still didn't budge. Finally she pulled the covers back.

"Get up, Kitty. Now!"

It was cold in that bedroom. Even lying in bed under the covers it was cold. If I moved only slightly, the sheets would be freezing where I hadn't lain. Sometimes I got dressed under the covers. But here she was pulling them off and beginning to shout at me.

I pulled the covers back over my head again. Now she tried a different tack, her voice almost caressing. "Dolly," she said. "Have a wash and come down for breakfast and we'll go."

I opened my eyes. "I'm not going back to Mrs. Barker, even if you told Dr. Hunt I was coming back this morning. I'm not going." And I began to cry.

My Mum went on and on at me. It seemed like forever. Finally she left, me still sobbing away, with my head deep down under the covers.

"I'll go and phone again," she said on the way out. "Perhaps Dr. Hunt will find you another billet. Will you go back then?"

"No!" I said.

"If it's a nice place, will you go back for my sake? I don't want anything to happen to you here, Kitty. I'm going to phone now."

I stayed in bed. I couldn't understand why she hadn't asked me exactly why I had come home so suddenly. She was so sure, I guess, that it was because of the housework. Even though Dr. Hunt had told her there was another reason and that I would explain, she was so busy making me go back that she didn't even ask. How strange mothers are! They never really listen, I thought. But I wouldn't go back. I was sure Dr. Hunt wouldn't find another place for me, and that I would be all right here.

I heard the shop bell clink and Uncle Yudi take down the shutters from the shop window. I heard my Mum bustling in the kitchen. But I didn't go down. After a while Uncle Yudi came up to my room.

"'ow are ya', girl?" he said. "She's makin' breakfast for ya downstairs. She can't phone Dr. Hunt until this afternoon, when your school starts."

I smiled to myself. That's good, I thought. The longer it takes her to phone, the longer I have to stay home.

"Tell Mummy that I'm so tired I just want to sleep a bit longer," I said.

He tousled my hair and plumped up my pillow.

"Go on, 'ave a little more sleep, girl," he said. "It'll make you feel better. And remember, I'm with you all the way."

He left. I curled up in a ball, nearly at the bottom of the bed, and fell asleep.

Again I was awakened, with the covers being pulled back.

"Well," my Mum said sharply. "I spoke to Dr. Hunt, not for too long as I didn't have any more coppers to put in the box. She said she would try to get you another place and that I should phone on Friday and she'd let me know. If there is another place, you'll go back on Sunday, no arguments, and that's that."

Please God, I prayed in my head, don't let her find me another place. Don't let me have to go back there.

104

Because I knew that if there was another place for me to go, there would be no more arguments. However much I cried, I would have to go back.

I wasn't very happy those next few days. I dreaded the phone call Mum would make. I stayed in the house mostly. There was no one to play with because everyone I knew was in the country. Sometimes I helped in the shop, sometimes I listened to the wireless, sometimes I read. I even wanted to try making doll furniture, but there weren't any match boxes around for it. I used to have fun doing that. I would pad the boxes with cotton wool, and then glue bits of material or old socks over them to make sofas and armchairs for a doll's house I once had. Still, I thought, whatever I'm doing now is better than going back to Bishop Stortford.

On Friday my Mum went back up the street to the phone box and came back quickly with the news that Dr. Hunt had found me a new place to stay, with some very nice people whose daughter was a Stortford girl. She went to school in the morning. I would go in the afternoon as usual. Dr. Hunt said she was my age and thought we would get on very well.

"No arguments now, Kitty" she said. "On Sunday we go. And we'll take an extra case so that I can go to the Barkers and get your things."

"But I'm not going with you to the Barkers," I said. "Not me!"

I wanted the next day to last forever.

Sunday morning came and I knew I couldn't fight

any more. We left the house early and when we arrived at Bishop Stortford it was cold, rainy and gloomy. Dr. Hunt had given my mother directions. We had to walk right to the other end of town from the Barkers, to a beautiful street, to the house of a family called Mendez. It was set back off the road, by itself. It was white, with broad steps going up to the front door. Smoke was coming out of the chimney. It looked like a house out of an old English painting.

I think my Mum was a bit nervous when she saw it. She clutched my hand tightly as we went up the wide steps. There was a brass knocker on the door and a brass letter box under it. My Mum reached up, still holding my hand, and knocked. We waited. My heart began to thump and I felt my knees begin to go funny as if I was going to fall down.

My Mum looked at me. "This is going to be lovely for you Kitty, you'll see."

I hoped so. But I also hoped nobody would be in so we could go back home.

No sooner had the thought entered my head than the door opened and a maid in a black dress with a little frilly white apron opened the door.

"May I speak to Mrs. Mendez?" my Mum said. "I believe she is expecting us."

The maid didn't ask us in. She just twisted on her heel without a word and disappeared. We waited outside. Finally she came back.

"Madam is expecting you," she said. "Please come in."

She led us into a large bright room. There was a lady sitting in a very large armchair. As we came in, she stood up and held out her hand to my Mum.

"Hello, Mrs. Simmonds," she said. "Dr. Hunt said you would be coming with your daughter today. Is this Kitty?" She turned to me. "I hope you'll be happy here. I have a daughter your age, you know."

Then she pulled a cord on the wall, and the maid came in.

"Mary, please take the girl up to her room. I want to talk to her mother. Then take her to the kitchen and give her a drink."

"Yes, Ma'am," said the maid. She looked at me. Was I supposed to go with her and leave my Mum? I looked at my Mum.

"Go, Kitty," my Mum said. "I'll see you before I leave. Don't worry! Mrs. Mendez and I just want to have a little chat. It's all right."

I didn't want to leave. But I knew I had to go. So, I followed the maid.

"Have you any cases?" she asked.

"No, just this satchel. But my Mum is going to my other place to get the rest of my clothes and then I'll have more."

She looked at me in a funny way and led me up the stairs to a small room at the back of the house. It was clean but not very bright. There was a bed, a chair, a small table and a cupboard, and a little window that overlooked the garden. Even though the trees were bare

107

and everything was drab and cold, I could see lots of sky and knew that at night I would be able to see the stars. I thought of the cat looking up at the moon. It made me feel better.

Mary waited while I took off my coat and hung up my new dress and put away the few other belongings I had brought. Then she took me down to the kitchen. Oh, what a lovely kitchen it was, all blue and white and so clean.

I sat down at the table.

"Do you come from London?" Mary asked.

"Yes," I said.

"What's it like there now? Any bombs?"

"No."

"Why did you come today? Were you kicked out of your other place?"

"No, I wasn't. I decided I wanted to go home."

"So why did you come back?"

"My Mum made me. Do you think I'll like it here?"

"I don't know. They have a daughter your age. But she's a bit uppish. And you'll have to eat here with me, I'm sure. She eats with her parents in the big dining room."

"Then why did they take me in here?" I asked, nervously.

"Oh, some teacher phoned up and said you had to have a place to go and Mrs. Mendez thought she should do her bit for the war effort, so she thought she'd take you. At least that's what I heard when I was serving one night. But I don't know if you're going to like it here. I'm sure Donna is not going to be too friendly. You should see her posh friends."

My stomach was turning already.

"Who are these people, the Mendezes, Mary?"

"The husband comes from Mexico, but the wife is English. They came back from Mexico just before the war. He's a scientist I think. Something in the government. Because of him we have very strange food here. It took me a while to get used to it myself. None of your steak and kidney pud! Hope you'll like it."

Mary poured me some milk and made me a cheese sandwich, not peculiar food to me. Perhaps she was just saying it. I wanted to like it here. But first I wanted to see my Mum.

Suddenly I heard a bell ring in the kitchen and it didn't sound like a telephone.

"What's that, Mary?"

"Oh, Madam wants me again. I'll be back in a minute." And she bustled out. What would happen next?

Soon I heard footsteps in the passage. My Mum and Mary came in, and my Mum threw her arms around me.

"You're going to be very happy here, Kitty," she said. "Mrs. Mendez is a very nice lady. Now I'm going to the Barkers to get your clothes. I'll be back as soon as I can. Don't worry, and just enjoy yourself here. Have you ever seen such a beautiful house?"

Before I knew it she had gone, her footsteps pattering down the passage, with Mary behind her. I heard the front door open, then close, and Mary quietly tripped back into the kitchen. This was my new home, but for how long?

Mary said I could go to my room, but I wanted some company and asked if I could stay until my Mum came back. She said I could if I didn't disturb her. She had to prepare the vegetables for dinner. So I sat quietly and watched her busy herself until I heard a loud knock on the front door. I knew it was my Mum. I sprang up wanting to go and open the door, but Mary said it was her job to do that.

I took my Mum up to my room. She had seen the Barkers, and they were very angry that I had run away without telling them. And yes, Sadie was still there. She wanted to see me. She had wanted to come back with my Mum but the Barkers wouldn't let her. I would see her in school tomorrow. I didn't really want to see her, or anyone from school for that matter. But I knew I would have to. I would make up some big stories to tell them, and then maybe they'd all want to run away like me. Of course I'd never tell my Mum this.

We unpacked the things my Mum had fetched from the Barkers and went back down to the kitchen. Mary made my Mum a cup of tea. I wanted to walk her back to the station, but she wouldn't let me. I might get lost coming back, she said. It wasn't the same direction as the Barkers, and it was getting dark. Next day I could explore on my way to school, she said, perhaps with Mrs. Mendez' daughter.

I said my goodbyes, a little surer things would be all

right. My Mum handed me some spending money as she left, and some treats she had been saving till now. Then I went back into the kitchen to talk to Mary.

"What's the daughter's name again, Mary?"

"Donna."

"Where is she?"

"Oh, at some birthday party. She has a lot of friends and is always going to parties and things. But she's expected home for dinner. Her mother or father will go and get her. They don't allow her to come home alone."

Presently there were footsteps in the passage and the kitchen door pushed open. Standing in the doorway was a girl my age, with long dark hair and lovely white skin. She looked at me.

"Are you the new evacuee?" she said. "My mother told me you were coming."

She didn't even come right into the kitchen, but just flung the words at me from the door. Then she turned to Mary.

"Mummy said I can have milk and biscuits now. Will you bring them to me in the morning room?" She closed the door and left as if she had never been there at all.

Mary looked at me. "I told you so," she said.

But perhaps when next we met it would be better.

I didn't want to leave the kitchen, or Mary. Yet I wanted to explore and see the rest of the house. I didn't know what to do. Somehow, I thought, the more questions I would ask Mary the worse things would sound. Perhaps I had better find out what the place was like on my own. What did Donna mean by the 'mourning' room? Was that where people go after someone has died? Or was it where you go in the morning? A very funny word to use for a room, I thought. But I knew if I asked Mary she would tell me something that wouldn't make sense to me. She had said the food was strange here but then had given me a cheese sandwich and glass of milk, and they weren't strange at all. So I decided to stay in the kitchen until Mary told me to leave. Perhaps I could even help her take something upstairs or help serve at the table. Maybe then I would see what this house was like.

"Mary," I said. "Can I help you with anything?"

"Oh no, dear. I can do everything myself. We have a daily. I do the cooking and serving. They used to have a cook but since the war they can't get the help they'd like. Our daily, Mrs. Herlie, comes in every morning. She's a nice old girl. You'll like her."

"So, when can I see the house, Mary? I was ever so scared when I first came in. I didn't really look around. And you were right, their girl isn't very friendly. But let me help you take something upstairs, Mary."

"All right, then. But don't go poking your nose into rooms that don't concern you. They'll go wild and so will I. And then you'll have to find another place to live."

Mary didn't have anything to take upstairs just then. After a while I said I would go to my room. But instead, my heart in my mouth, I walked quietly down the passage. I hadn't realized how long and wide it was when I first came in. Mum and I had hurried from the front door to the room where we met Mrs. Mendez. There were great big pictures on the walls of the passage, all dark in gold frames. The main room where we had met Mrs. Mendez was quiet. There were lights on, and I could smell wood burning in the fireplace. I didn't poke my head in, though. I was afraid someone would see me.

I wondered where Donna was. And where was the 'mourning' room, whatever that was? I wandered down the passage and looked at the great big pictures of old people sitting in big chairs. Then I saw another room, all pretty, with flowered sofas and little tables. Sitting on one of those sofas was Donna. I crept in.

"Hello, Donna," I said.

"Oh. Hello. What's your name, anyway?"

"Kitty."

"Oh yes, I remember, the evacuee. You shouldn't be in here you know."

"Oh? Why not?"

"It's not for you."

"But I thought . . . perhaps . . . we could be friends," I said.

"Friends?" she said. "I don't know about that. But I do know you shouldn't be in here. You should be in the kitchen with Mary. I'd better ask my mother whether you can come in here again."

"Why can't I come in here? Why can't I sit here the same as you?"

"This is not your house. You come from the slums,

from the slums of London I'm told. It's very different here."

"It really is different, Donna," I said. And I put my head in the air.

Oh, how angry I was! I knew where I came from. I didn't need her to remind me. But my Mum always used to tell me: "Kitty, hold your head high." I never really knew what she meant until now. I wasn't going to show this girl, who thought she was who knows what, that I was upset. The slums were lovely. They were warm and friendly. Not like here.

20

Big Decisions

WHAT WAS I GOING to do now? How long could I talk to Mary in the kitchen? I went out of that 'mourning' room up to my bedroom, lay on my bed, and winked at the stars.

It would be all right, I thought, and if it wasn't I would just go home again. I still had my spending money. But my mother would be wild. I only came back because of her. I had to go to school tomorrow and I didn't want to do that either. Well, I would see what tomorrow would bring.

I fell asleep thinking about it all. I was sure I wouldn't sleep, but I must have slept a long time. I awoke to the sound of heavy rain pounding on the window pane. Everything looked so bare and bleak and wet outside.

The sky was heavy with dark clouds. I didn't know what time it was. There was no clock in the room, and I didn't own a wristwatch.

What was there to get up for anyway? Now there was no charring to rush through. I didn't have any homework. I didn't want to write to my Mum, at least until I'd been to school. But I got out of bed. The floor was so cold under my feet. I got dressed quickly. The house was quiet and I couldn't hear anybody. I crept down the wide carpeted stairs to the hall. The best place to go would be the kitchen. Maybe Mary would tell me the time. I pushed open the door and went in and there was Mary.

" 'ello, dear," she said. "I went up to wake you hours ago, but you looked so peaceful sleeping I thought it was a shame to wake you on your first day, so I let you sleep. But not tomorrow, my girl. It's up with everyone else!"

"What time is it, Mary?" I asked.

"Nearly 'alf past nine."

"Isn't anybody in the house?"

"Oh no! Donna's gone to school. Madam took her, and then she has to go to some kind of war meeting. You'd better have some breakfast now, dear. You go to a Jewish place for lunch, don't you? That's what I was told. I hope they give you a good lunch. Don't know about that kind of food. Very different from the English, I'm told. No steak and kidney pud, I bet."

I didn't know what she was talking about and just let her go on.

"We don't have much English food here either. All

Mexican stuff, rice and curry and lots of bananas. You'll have to have some when you come back from school."

She put my breakfast on the table as she talked on and on.

"It's so quiet here, Mary," I got in finally. "And I really thought I could be friends with Donna."

"I didn't think so," she said. "But you can come in here sometimes. Not too often though. I have things to do. You'll come here for your meals and then do what you have to do in your room. And you mustn't come down late for breakfast. I like to do all the breakfasts at the same time. So I'll give you a clock."

"Can't I eat breakfast with the family?" I asked.

"Of course not. You have to eat in here with me."

I choked.

I thanked Mary for breakfast and went back to my room. It was too early to go to school, and raining too hard to wander and explore the garden. So I stayed in my room for what seemed forever, and then found my Wellingtons and Mac and set out. I trudged into town, the town I had left and hoped never to see again. The Mendez' house was further away from town than the Barkers had been and it took me a long time to get to the High Street. Streams of water flowed in the gutters. The few cows I saw in the fields seemed to shiver in the damp.

On the High Street itself everything was the same. I dragged my way to the communal kosher kitchen. Even though it was early I was sure some of the helpers would be there. They were, and were glad to see me.

"Where have you been, Kitty?" Mrs. Singer asked. "Have you been ill? I asked Sadie where you were and she wouldn't tell me."

"I went home for a while," I said. "Wanted to see my Mum and to see how London was. It was lovely. I know I'm early but can I stay and wait for the girls?"

"Of course, dear," Mrs. Singer said. "Was London quiet? Did your Mum make you come back?" I just shrugged my shoulders. In no time at all I heard voices and lots of laughter and the girls bustled through the door. The first one to see me was Big Mouth Maddie Levene. She barged past the other girls.

"Where have you been?" she asked. "We heard you were expelled. How come you're back?"

"I wasn't expelled," I said. "I ran away. And it was wonderful. You should do it sometime."

"Really!" she said. "Tell us about it."

"Some time," I said. I didn't really want to speak to any of them and yet I wanted company. I didn't know what I wanted. Suddenly I saw Sadie. She came running over to the table and threw her arms around me.

"Oh, Kitty!" she said. "I'm so glad to see you. I'm so glad you're back. I was so upset when you ran away and didn't even tell me."

"You wouldn't have come with me. You told me so. So I had to do it all by myself. I didn't want to come back. But my Mum made me. And I don't want to stay."

"How was it in London?"

I thought of all the things I wanted to say. But I said,

117

"Oh, it was lovely. On the train going home I met lots of lovely people. Airmen and airwomen. They gave me chocolates and sweets. London was lovely and quiet. Everybody was so glad to see me. I had such a good time. So much better than here. And there was no school . . . and no charring. It was wonderful. But my Mum was scared of bombs. So here I am."

Where are you staying?" Sadie asked.

"With posh people from Mexico. They have a beautiful big house. And a lovely daughter who's my friend. I only came yesterday but she's ever so nice to me."

"Can I meet her?" Sadie asked.

"Well, you can't come to the house. They're ever so posh and I don't think they'll let anybody else in. I was special so they took me."

I don't think Sadie believed me but I didn't know what else to say. I wasn't going to tell her how miserable it was there. It was miserable at the Barkers. I didn't want to show her I was unhappy again.

She was glad to see me though and I was happy for that. We went to school arm in arm. I asked her when she was going home again.

"Oh, Kitty," she said, "I just can't do what you do. I don't know. I still have to do housework, but not as much as before. And Mrs. Barker is trying to be nicer. At first I was scared that I would have to make up for both of us."

Then Sadie told me how lonely it was without me. There was nobody else in the billet. Her Mum wouldn't

118

let her come home and she just didn't have the pluck, she said, to hop on a train like I did. She thought she was stuck there for the duration. I think she admired me a little bit. And that made me feel good.

I went to see Dr. Hunt before going to class, as I had promised my Mum I would. She said she was glad I had come back and hoped I would be happy in my new billet. She really was a nice lady.

School was the same as before. At the end of the day I trudged back to the Mendez', stomping on all the rainbows in the puddles. Thank goodness I didn't have to eat supper there, just tea, since I had my big meal at lunch time. I went to the back door, put my Wellingtons and Mac in the scullery, and started for the kitchen. Donna was just coming out. She saw me.

"Hello, Donna," I said. She just glanced at me and walked away. She didn't even say hello.

I went into the kitchen.

"Hello, Mary," I said. "I'm back." The air in the kitchen had a strange smell.

"'ello, luv. It's high tea today. Curried rice and bananas."

"Curried rice and bananas! Is that the funny smell?"

"Not funny at all, dear. Just Mexican. Takes a bit of time to get used to. You Jews have different foods and so do the Mexicans. You'll get used to it."

"But I had my dinner at lunch time," I said.

"Well, that's all there is. Or you can have some bread and jam."

"I'll try the rice and bananas, Mary."

It was awful. It made my mouth so hot. What did they put in it? I would just have to finish it. But tomorrow it would be bread and jam. Thank goodness I've got all those treats my Mum had given me, I thought.

And so the days went. That whole week nobody in that whole house spoke to me, except Mary. By Saturday I knew I couldn't stand it any longer. But this time I wasn't going to be silly and run away without telling anybody. The only person I wouldn't tell would be my Mum. I would leave a note for Dr. Hunt. And I would tell the Mendezes that I was going to London to see my Mum.

21

The Last Farewell

I COULDN'T SLEEP the next Friday night. I tossed and turned thinking about the loneliness of that whole week. I had made friends with Sadie again. And all the girls at school were talking to me as they had been before. But in this house nobody talked to me except Mary who didn't like me bothering her. Donna always put her nose in the air if she saw me and never said a word. Mr. and Mrs. Mendez were seldom there. There wasn't even a dog to talk to and I didn't even like dogs. We'd never had one at home.

The war could go on forever, I thought. My Mum and Dad could be killed. But I would have to stay in this house, where no one talked, until I died. The thought was horrible.

I pulled back the blackout curtains and looked up at the sky. It had been a cold clear day. Tonight the sky was full of stars, I thought, twinkling some message to me. I tried to find the Milky Way to make the time pass, twisting my head this way and that till I tired myself out. I climbed back into bed, but sleep wouldn't come.

Why not just get up and go home now? But it was no use going to the station in the middle of the night. There wouldn't be any trains running. And I had decided that if I did go back to London everyone would know—except my mother.

I got out of bed again and packed a few things in my satchel, all ready for the morning. My Mum would just have to come back for the rest of my things as she had before. I put in my sweets to eat on the train, eating a few while I was packing. I was all ready. In the morning I would be off.

It must still be a few hours till morning, I thought. So I tried to sleep again. And this time I did. When I opened my eyes it looked like it was going to be another nice day. I dressed quickly and went down to the kitchen.

"Well, you're up bright and early, dear," Mary said. "But you've got rings under your eyes. Didn't you sleep well?"

"No, Mary, I didn't." I said. "I'm too excited."

"What about, dear?"

"Didn't I tell you Mary? You know I had a letter from

my Mum. She wants me to come home for the weekend. My Dad is coming home. She sent me fare money. Is Mrs. Mendez up yet? I want to tell her and then get going so I can make the early train."

"Oh no, luv. Mrs. Mendez went up to London last night with the Master. She won't be back until Monday at least."

"Oh!" I said. "Well, can you please tell her?" Then I remembered that I would be back by Monday. "Oh, but of course," I stammered, "I'll be able tell her myself."

Mary looked at me suspiciously. "Are you sure your Mum said that? Or are you just playing a trick on us and leaving like you did the last billet? Perhaps I should phone Dr. Hunt and tell her."

"Oh no, Mary," I said. "Dr. Hunt knows. I told her yesterday." My heart was thumping so hard I was sure Mary could hear it.

"I'd better go now Mary. I'd like to get home early. My Mum said she would meet me at Liverpool Street Station. I don't want to keep her waiting."

I held my breath. What would Mary say now?

"All right," she said finally. "I'll make you a sandwich for the train."

I couldn't believe how easy this was. It must be my lucky day. I ate breakfast and went upstairs for my satchel. I was glad I was only taking that little bag. Otherwise Mary would be more suspicious than she was already. I kissed her goodbye and said I would see her Monday morning. Then I left that house. I hoped it would be forever. No, I knew it would be forever.

I had written a note to Dr. Hunt telling her I was going home because I hated being so lonely and thanked her for all she had done for me. I hurried to school to find the caretaker. I would ask him to give the note to her on Monday, praying that she wouldn't be around the school on a Saturday morning.

The streets were deserted, the school playground empty. I ran round the back to the caretaker's cottage and knocked. There was no reply. What a stroke of luck! I couldn't believe it. Nobody was home. I could just put the note in the letterbox and he wouldn't be able to ask me any questions. I poked the letter through and left quickly, not even looking back in case he would appear. I didn't want to run. I just walked as quickly as I could.

It was market day in town. Everyone was rushing about so my rushing was nothing unusual, thank goodness. It was cold but sunny. By the time I got to the station I was sweating. I stopped outside to catch my breath. And then I saw her. There, going into the station, was my form mistress, Miss Harris. I thought I would faint.

I turned and quickly walked away from the station. Then I saw a siding and sat down with my back against the wall to wait. Would she come out again? Was she waiting for someone? Or was she going to London, too? What should I do?

I waited and waited. She didn't come out. After what seemed forever a train chugged into the station. I wanted to get on that train so badly. But if she saw me, that would be the end of my running away. I would just have to take the next train. I heard the hustle and bustle inside the station. My eyes, though, were glued to the entrance. She didn't come out. Finally the porter blew his whistle, the train began huffing and puffing, chug-chugging away. Still no Miss Harris. She must be on the train. I prayed that nobody I knew would turn up for the next train. I supposed I would have a long wait.

I sat by the siding wall until there was no sound of the train left. Then I gingerly walked into the empty booking office. The station master must have recognized me from the last time.

" 'ello, ducks," he said. "You goin' 'ome again?"

I smiled up at him. "Yes. My Dad's home for the weekend. My Mum sent me fare money to come and see him. It's been such a long time."

"Well, you just missed the train, ducks. One of your teachers was on it. Pity! You could have gone with her and had some company. Now you're on your own. The next train isn't for a couple of hours. Why don't you go back to your billet and come back then?"

"Oh no. No one's at home. I'll just sit here and wait. I've got homework to do anyway."

"Well," he said, "perhaps another one of your teachers will come and you can travel with her."

I shuddered. Just suppose Dr. Hunt would show up. Oh no, I thought. No!

"Oh dear," I said, "I've left my homework in my billet. I'll run back and get it so I can do it on the train."

"You've lots of time, ducks," he said. "Next train won't be 'ere for a couple of hours."

I ran back to my hiding place behind the siding. With my back to the wall I kept my eyes glued to the station entrance to wait for the train. No other teachers came, and none of the girls either. Just older people. And some soldiers, going back to barracks I supposed, and an airman with his arm around a lady who was pushing a pram. She was crying. He must be going away for a long time I thought. He looked so sad.

Nobody noticed me, thank goodness. I took out my sandwiches and ate one or two. They helped pass the time. Mary had made me a really nice lunch and I was feeling bad already for lying to her. Perhaps I would write to her when I got home. I didn't touch my sweets though. I wanted to save them for the train.

Time passed quickly because before I knew it I heard the train puffing in the distance. I ran into the booking office and asked for a half fare to London. Nobody I knew was around.

"Return or single?" the clerk asked.

"Single, please," I whispered, scared that the station master would hear me and remember that I told him I was just going for the weekend.

There. It was done. I was leaving forever. My Mum wouldn't die without me. We would be together forever and ever.

The platform darkened as the train came into the station. Doors flung open. I walked along the platform to the farthest compartment, my head held high this time. No good to be too near the entrance, I thought. A teacher could suddenly spring in at the last moment.

The porter blew his whistle, doors slammed, and the train started huffing and puffing down the track to wonderful, wonderful London. Goodbye Bishop Stortford! Goodbye Mr. and Mrs. Mendez and horrible Donna! Goodbye Sadie and Dr. Hunt! I'm on my way, Mummy. And this time you won't make me come back!

I curled up in my corner seat and smiled to myself. I had done it!

22

A Ghostly Welcome

THERE WERE A COUPLE of soldiers in the compartment, and an old lady and gentleman dressed in their best, or so it looked to me. She was in a little hat with a spotted veil covering her eyes, and he was holding her hand. It seemed funny to see old people holding hands. They looked at me, and the lady said, "Where are you going all by yourself on a train?"

I smiled. "I'm going back to London for the weekend to see my Dad. He's coming home on leave. My Mum told me to come."

"She allowed you to go by yourself?" she asked.

"Oh yes. I go everywhere by myself. I even take my

little brother and sister with me. We're all evacuated to Bishop Stortford. But my Mum said I was the only one who could go home as I'm the oldest."

Then I plucked up courage and asked, "Are you going to a wedding or something? You look so dressed up."

"Oh no," the gentleman said. "We're going to see our son off. He's going overseas and we want him to see us looking our best. We don't know if he'll ever see us again." They looked at each other and I thought I saw tears in their eyes.

So everyone is thinking that someone they love may die . . . just like I did about my Mum and Dad. Now I knew it was right for me to go home and be with my Mum, forever.

The door of the compartment opened and the ticket collector came in. Somehow I wasn't scared this time. I showed him my ticket without my heart playing leap frog as it had done the last time.

A couple of airmen got in at the next station and started talking to the soldiers, offering them and then me some chocolates. The time went by so quickly that before I knew it the train pulled into Liverpool Street Station with a lot of jolts and jerks. Now for the fireworks I thought. What was my Mum going to say and do?

"Hope your son's all right," I said to the old couple, and hurried down the train corridor to an open door onto the platform. As I passed the ticket collector, I saw a tall young airman rushing up to the old couple.

I ran up the stairs, through the station, over the

bridge, and out into Bishopsgate. The paperseller was outside as usual, and across the street was Dirty Dick's, the pub, with orange peel and paper littering the doorway. Everyone was hurrying and scurrying around as usual on a Saturday afternoon. I crossed over, hurried down Middlesex Street, through Half Moon Passage to Commercial Street, past 'Itchy' Park where the tramps were still sitting on the benches, and round the back to my street. Being the Sabbath, the shop was closed. The shutters were up. The street was quiet. I went to the front, and pushed open the heavy shop door. The shop was dark but I could see by the light from the kitchen.

"Mummy," I called. "Mummy."

I heard her say to my uncle: "Yudi. I thought I heard Kitty's voice."

"Passie, are you mad? She's in the country. It's your nerves again. I told you to go and see about 'em. Sam's away. Kitty's away. It makes you so nervous. You sound like Joan of Arc, 'earing voices."

"Mummy," I called again.

"Yudi," she said, "I hear it again."

"So go to the door and see what you're driving me mad about."

She opened the door of the kitchen and peered into the dark shop.

"Mummy. It's me." And I ran to her.

"Kitty!" she screamed. Then she quickly pulled herself together. "Kitty, what are you doing home? You're supposed to be in the country, away from all this." But she hugged me and pulled me into the kitchen. My Uncle Yudi was standing there with a big grin on his face.

"So you did it again, girl," he said. "I'm so glad you're back."

"Sit down," my Mum said. "Yudi, put on the kettle! What's going on, Kitty? Why are you here? Did they send you home? What did you do? Nobody told me you were coming." And she went on and on.

"I came home to stay, Mummy. And I'm not going back. Never!"

I didn't think she even heard what I said, because all she was doing was kissing me. She seemed in a real state. Uncle Yudi made the tea and brought out some cake. We drank and ate and for a while nobody spoke.

My uncle finally broke the silence.

"Don't you feel better, Passie, now that she's 'ome?"

"I can't believe it, Yudi. But she has to go back."

They were talking as if I wasn't there.

"You've been worrying all this time, Passie," my uncle said. "Been 'aving a real carry on, you 'ave. And now she's 'ome and you want 'er to go back. Passie, you know, you should've 'ad more than one child. You dote on 'er too much."

She put her arms around me again and started to cry.

"I want you safe, Kitty," she said. "I don't care about myself. Well, we'll talk about it later. Drink your tea and have some cake. It's Yudi's favourite currant cake. Thank goodness it's still quiet in London. But who knows when we'll have a raid."

Then she turned to my uncle.

"Yudi, it's nearly blackout time. Pull the curtains. Thank God you got here before blackout, Kitty. Oh, you are a naughty girl, you know."

She seemed to be jumbling everything up in her excitement. But I didn't care. I was home and that was all that mattered to me.

I looked round the kitchen. We did almost everything in this room except sleep, and my uncle even did that sometimes. We washed here. We ate our meals here. We entertained here. There was always a fire burning in the grate. We never sat around in any other room. The whole room was about half the size of Mary's kitchen. But it was so warm here. Everyone was always talking. It would be nice to have a carpet. But no matter. Tibby was still here though all the kittens had been given away. She came over and wound her tail around my legs and looked up at me with her big green eyes, and her whiskers twitched as if to say, "I'm glad you're home too."

I felt warm and wonderful. I would stay here forever.

23

Determination

THE CAT'S WHISKERS tickling my cheeks woke me up in the morning. The room was very dark. The blackout curtain hadn't been pulled back. But I heard bustling downstairs.

I didn't want to get up and face the nagging about going back again. I wasn't going to go.

"Scat, Tibby," I said. "Go away." But Tibby meowed and purred and jumped up on my bed. I rolled toward the wall. The part I hadn't slept on was freezing cold so I rolled back to where I had been all night. There it was warm. I covered my head with the blanket to snuggle down again. Just putting my nose out in this house made me freeze. But it was home. I knew there would be a fight with my Mum. I knew she would try to make me go back. But this time I was determined. Determined to stay.

I tried to think of what to do. And then it came to me. My eyes. I hated wearing glasses. My Mum was always saying that if I cry too much my eyes will get worse. I couldn't believe it. How could tears make eyes worse? But that's what my Mum thought. And that's what Uncle Yudi had kept reminding her last night. ("Stop screaming at her and making her cry, Passie! Her eyes will get worse!") If that's what they thought, I would cry until she stopped nagging. She wouldn't go on too long if she knew it would hurt me. I smiled to myself, my head still under the blankets, Tibby still on my bed. I slept some more.

I didn't hear her come up the stairs. But the next thing I knew a grey watery light was coming through the window and then I heard my Mum's voice: "Kitty, where are you?" She prodded the bed. "Are you so cold? It's almost afternoon, Kitty. You must really have needed that sleep. But you have to get up now so you can get

131

ready to go back later today."

Here it comes, I thought. But don't cry yet!

"I'm ever so tired Mum. And this is the most comfortable bed in the whole world. If I curl up I don't feel the cold."

"Did the hot water bottle leak?" She had put it in my bed the night before. Now it felt cold and rubbery at the bottom of the bed.

"It didn't leak, Mum," I said. "I'll come down soon."

"I'll make you a nice lunch and pack some things for you to take back. Don't be long." And she hustled down the stairs.

I turned over. Then I heard my uncle's door open. He poked his head into my room. He hadn't shaved and his chin was all bristles. But, as always, he had a big grin on his face.

"What's the story this time, girl?"

"Uncle Yudi, I'm home for good. This time she won't make me go back. Will you stick up for me? My Dad isn't here to help me."

"Of course, girl. I'll work on your Mum. You know how she 'ates you to cry. So you just turn on the water works and between us we'll keep you 'ere. But I 'eard 'er say she's making you a nice lunch. So go down and keep on 'er good side. It'll work out, you'll see. Pity there are no schools open in London. It would be easier for you then. But I'll tell 'er I'll learn you, bloody laugh that'll be! Anyway, you can 'elp in the shop. You like to read and the libraries are open. You'll be all right 'ere. Even if the bombs come, you and your Mum can run to the shelter. I'll look after the 'ouse and see that Jerry doesn't bomb it."

"Uncle Yudi," I laughed. "You are funny. If a bomb is headed for this house what can you do?"

"Listen, Kitty. A bomb only comes when your number's on it. And it only comes to the good ones. I'm no bloody good so it won't 'it me."

"Oh, Uncle Yudi!"

"'urry girl. Downstairs with you. Let's start the fireworks up and get 'em over and done with."

He lurched off to his room. I got right up, dressed, washed in the sink on the landing, and went downstairs. Tibby followed behind, nearly tripping me trying to wind her tail around my legs.

"Smells good, Mum," I said as I entered the kitchen. She was standing over the cooker, frying fish in bubbling hot oil in our large black iron frying pan.

"Fish and chips, Mum?" I asked.

"Well, it's too late for breakfast. So we'll have a big lunch and you can take some fish back to the Mendezes. I bought it fresh this morning in the Lane."

"Can we have latkes with it, Mum?"

"Oh yes, and chips as well."

How wonderful to be home! Latkes. I hadn't had them in ages. They were made from leftover egg and matzah meal batter for the fish. She would drop spoonfuls into the hot oil, fry them to a golden brown, and serve them with sugar. Yum! This was home. The arguments could wait. Presently, Uncle Yudi came down.

He must have smelled the fried fish.

"'Aven't you fed the girl yet, Passie?" he said. "You're starving 'er almost as much as they are in the country, poor kid. 'ungry there, now 'ungry 'ere." He turned to me. "Do you ever have fish and chips in that fancy house, Kitty?" he asked. "Or are they too posh for that?"

"No Uncle, I don't! Sometimes we have it in the communal kitchen. But not latkes, of course. I can't wait for them."

"Well stop starving 'er, Passie. Let's fatten 'er up!" His grin widened.

"Just wait, Yudi," she said. "This takes time. Have a cup of tea or open the shop or something till I'm ready. Kitty, go and help him. You should have been down much earlier, Yudi. I can't do everything: look after your shop, and the house as well."

"Oh well," my uncle said. "Kitty's 'ere now and she can do the shop, and then you'll stop grumbling at me all the time. She can serve the whole week, and I'll do Sundays. There's no horse racing then."

"Kitty's going back and there's to be no argument about that." I didn't say a word. Let them argue first, I thought. Later it would be my turn.

Finally we had lunch and then my Mum began to pack up some fish for the Mendezes. Or so she thought.

"You'll get the train back before it gets dark, Kitty," she said.

"No Mum, not this time!"

"Oh, stop it!" she said. "We're not going to have that

134

again like last time."

"No, Mum! I've told them I'm not going back."

"I don't understand you, Kitty. You're in a beautiful house with lovely people. There's even a girl your own age there. And a maid so you don't have to do any housework. I'm sure that Sadie would be only too glad to be in a place like that. So why are you giving me all this worry?"

"Yes, Mum, it's ever so posh. But that Donna won't even talk to me. Every time she sees me she turns her head away. She eats with her Mum and Dad and I have to eat with Mary in the kitchen. Mary's the only one who talks to me. And she's always busy. So no one, no one talks to me in that house and I hate it. And all they ever eat is curried rice and bananas! So I'm staying here and that's that."

"But you are going, my child, you are," she said.

The argument began. When I had planned the tears, I thought I would have to pretend to cry. But with her nagging and with her excitement, I began to get really upset, and real tears came and they wouldn't stop. My uncle kept butting in with, "Do you want 'er to ruin 'er eyes, Passie? If she keeps on crying, she'll ruin 'er eyes." And my Mum saying, "Stop crying! And Yudi, stop interfering." It went on and on. But the first round had been won, I could tell.

My tears and her anger subsided and finally she told me to go and play outside. There were no children on the street so I wandered round and poked my head into a street shelter. It had a horrible smell of cats, but no cats

135

were there. I felt free—for a little while anyway.

My Mum was angry when I came in, but didn't say anything more. Before I went to bed, she said we would talk about the country tomorrow. She looked tired and worried. My uncle had gone out and the house was quiet, but this was home and a different kind of quietness. This was my house, not a stranger's.

Next day there was the same argument, and I shed more tears. Another day won. By Thursday my Mum had given in. She went to the phone box at the end of the street to ask Mrs. Mendez if she could come for my clothes on Sunday. Then she phoned Dr. Hunt to tell her that I definitely wouldn't be back.

On Saturday we went to see Sadie's Mum to see if there was anything my Mum could take down to her. Just like my Mum that was, always thinking of someone else! Mrs. Davidovitch thought I was very wild, coming home alone. Her Sadie wouldn't do a thing like that, she said, adding that my Mum should have made me go back. We were both sorry we had gone to see her.

My evacuation to the country was finally over. But now the fear of what would happen next would start. Would the air raids start soon? Would I be killed? Or was all this a phony war, as I had heard people say? But I was home and I didn't care. There must be some children around. Not everyone could be in the country. I would find them. I knew the neighbourhood. For now, I was happy.

24

Toynbee Hall

BOTH MUM AND I got up early that Sunday morning, she to go to the country and me to help in the shop. Uncle Yudi, of course, didn't come down early. Mum said he had come home very late the night before. He always did on Saturday nights. Mum said he was always out with the boys, except he didn't look like a boy to me. He was little, and wiry and tough. Mum said that if anyone would start with him he would give them what for. She said he had even fought Oswald Mosley with the Aldgate Boys a few years before when the Blackshirts came to Stepney and tried to attack the Jews. She told me that he was once a featherweight jockey but he'd had a fight with his manager who had called him a dirty Jew. That was the end of his being a jockey, so now he played the horses instead of riding them. I didn't mind him sleeping late. I promised Mum I would wake him if the shop got busy, which it never did.

The only person who came into the shop that morning was Mrs. Ginsberg. I felt important serving her. I ladled milk from the churn into her half pint glass bottle and made sure the lid fit properly so that it would not spill, as my Mum had taught me. She only wanted two ounces of butter, but I still used the wooden pats to make a little square, slapped it on greaseproof paper as I had seen Uncle Yudi do it, and then tipped it on the scale. She didn't have money to pay so I had to mark her down in Uncle Yudi's book.

Wasn't this better than going to school in the country!

My Mum didn't come back until the evening and she didn't look very happy. She said the suitcase was heavy and it took a long time to carry it from the station. Uncle Yudi put the kettle on as soon as she sat down.

"It was a hard day, eh Passie?" he said. "Were all the girls sorry Kitty has come 'ome?"

"I'm glad I went," my Mum said. "Those Mendezes did us a whole favour to take Kitty in. But they didn't even know she had come home. They may be rich but they don't have any heart. The only nice one was the maid. She told me to give you a hug from her, Kitty, and to drop her a line. Mary said she had given Mrs. Mendez your letter but the lady hadn't even bothered to read it. Too busy being posh, I suppose. I didn't see Sadie. I didn't want to go back to the Barkers. I thought I might see her on the High Street. But I did go to your school, and what a bit of luck. Dr. Hunt was there. She was ever so nice. She's sorry you won't be coming back. And she wishes you luck."

My Mum put her arms around me.

"Kitty," she said, "I'm glad you're home, even after all the rows we've had. We'll pray there won't be any bombs. But if there are, we'll all go up together. Pity your Dad's not here. He'll be back when he finishes with the army huts. Let's hope it won't be long."

Tears welled up in her eyes, and she wiped her glasses.

138

"I should have had more children, Kitty," she said. "To put everything on one child is hard."

I let her cry and cuddled closer.

"It's all right Mum," I said. "I'll look after you." And I could see Uncle Yudi smiling, too.

And so the weeks went by, Mummy and I running the shop during the week and Uncle Yudi on Sunday. On Saturday, being the Sabbath, the shop was closed, and sometimes in the afternoon I would go to the library in Whitechapel High Street. One day the librarian told me that some classes would be opening at Toynbee Hall for children who had come back from evacuation. It was a settlement house not too far from the library.

I still hadn't seen any children around, at least none of my friends from the street. But there must be some or there wouldn't be a school opening. My Mum was so pleased when I told her. Her face beamed.

"Well thank goodness, Kitty," she said, "At last. I want you to have some education so you won't end up a dressmaker like Theresa." That seemed to me a strange thing for her to say. Theresa made herself lovely clothes and she'd even shown me how to make dolls' clothes. What was so terrible about being a dressmaker?

"How often will these classes be, Kitty?" she said, "Did you ask?"

"No, Mum, but when I go to the library again I'll go into Toynbee Hall and find out."

"Oh, I'll go. I'll go," she said. I think she must have been scared that I wouldn't go.

I had passed Toynbee Hall many times. Its back door was just at the bottom of Petticoat Lane, and the front door was on Commercial Street, opposite the police station. I had never been inside Toynbee. Whenever I had peered in on my way past, it had looked to me like an old church or a cloister with its arched entranceway. My Mum said that Oxford and Cambridge men had started it to teach people in Whitechapel about music and art and literature. They had classes on all the arts. And you could even get legal advice there too if you needed it. She said Youth Hostels had started there too. So even though she had never had the time for the luxury of classes there, she said, she was happy that I would be able to go.

She found out that classes would be held every morning for three hours and would start in April, right after Easter. But we would have to bring our own school books. So, if there were no air raids I could look forward to school and new friends in a few weeks.

Those weeks passed quickly. Just before Easter my Mum took me to enroll. We walked through to the cloistered courtyard in the centre of the building and came upon a dingy little door marked 'Warden.' We knocked and were invited in. Inside a man was bent over a desk which was covered with all kinds of papers. He stood up when he saw us and a big smile lit up his face. He introduced himself as Mr. Richardson. He was so tall his head almost touched the low ceiling.

"You've come to register for our school classes?" he said, holding out his hand. "How wonderful! You're our third pupil." He looked like the happy giant.

"I hope she'll be a good student," my Mum said.

"Why ever wouldn't she be?" he asked in his posh accent. "We'll certainly do the best we can. We're hoping for ten children in each class. Better than doing nothing. If things stay quiet we'll have other things for children to do, too. We're hoping to start Guides and Scouts again." He looked at my Mum. "Don't worry, Mother! Your daughter's going to love Toynbee. Didn't want to stay in the country, I suppose? Well, I don't blame her. There's no place like home. Anyway, we'll expect you the day after Easter Monday. Nine o'clock sharp. Be sure to bring school books, and we'll see what we can do to keep you up with your work. There'll be lots for you here at Toynbee. Let's just hope it doesn't get bombed."

He took us to the door and saw us out into the courtyard. There were a few benches there and flower beds with daffodils coming through.

"Look Mum, flowers in the middle of London!" We didn't have any on our street. The buildings around the courtyard were of old grey stone. My Mum said at one time it must have been a church or convent or something like that.

We went through a swing door at the back of the courtyard to get to Petticoat Lane. But everything behind that door was modern, just like my old school. They even had a lift. We walked up the stairs to have a look around. My Mum didn't like lifts much, or anything modern for that matter. She expected everything to be dingy and dirty here. But it wasn't. In fact it was clean as a pin everywhere. One of the doors we passed was marked 'Seventh North Stepney Girl Guides.' I wanted to go in, but my Mum wouldn't let me.

"Enough, Kitty," she whispered, "you'll get yourself in trouble before you even start. Wait 'til your classes begin before you poke around." She pulled me back down the stairs. On our way we passed a door marked 'Theatre' and another that said 'Stage Door.' I was thrilled. This was really something to look forward to. And who knows who I would meet.

25

Passover

THAT YEAR Passover and Easter came at the same time, and I was glad of that because I didn't want to miss any school days because of the Jewish holiday.

Usually I was sorry when Passover and Easter came together because there were so many wonderful Easter things we couldn't eat then. That made me feel especially different even though we lived in a mainly Jewish neighbourhood.

Other years, when I walked with my friends along Whitechapel High Street, the sweets department at Woolworths at the corner of Commercial Street was full of lovely chocolate Easter eggs. Dark chocolate eggs, trimmed with pink and white sugar roses and a yellow furry chicken just popping out, looking almost real. Yummy milk chocolate eggs decorated with satin ribbons sitting in a little wicker basket that seemed almost ready to hatch. And little marzipan eggs in silver paper. Those are the ones I always bought with the few pennies my Mum gave me.

Then we would walk past a bakery and the smell of the hot cross buns would waft through the air, spicy and sweet. How I would drool over them! But we couldn't eat any leaven during Passover week so all we could do was stand and stare.

I loved our house at Passover. My Mum worked so hard cleaning and polishing for the Seders. The whole family would come, like my mother's two sisters and my cousin Margy. My mother would prepare a special meal and the table would be laid with a snowy white cloth and silver candlesticks would gleam holding the tall white holiday candles.

Theresa and I wouldn't have a row that night, and my Mum and Dad would be nice to each other, and Uncle Yudi would make jokes.

Sometimes, though, my Mum would get upset with Uncle Yudi because instead of reading from the Haggadah about the exodus of the Jews from Egypt where they were slaves, he would try and be funny. He would mumble to himself, just loud enough for us to hear, "Ten to one on Moonbeam" or "Six to four the field." My Mum would glare at him and Theresa and I would laugh and we would lose our place in the Haggadah. My Dad would just continue as if nothing had happened.

We would have our meal—not in the kitchen as we always did, even on Friday nights, but upstairs in the front room. My Mum would get out her best china which she only used for Passover. I could never understand why we would use our very best just one week of the year, but she said that Passover was special.

Three matzahs, the unleavened bread, would be in a pile underneath the special embroidered cloth that my grandmother had made many years before. Before the meal began, my Dad would break the middle matzah and hand it around with bitter herbs and horseradish to remember the hardships in Egypt. How the horseradish would make our eyes sting when we took a big bite of it in between two pieces of matzah! When we complained, my Dad would say it was to remind us of the tears our ancestors had shed. Our life is too easy now, he would say.

The youngest person in the room—that was me— would recite certain parts of the service and my Dad would answer questions about the exodus of the Jews from Egypt when the Pharaohs reigned. It was wonderful . . . always a warm, cozy, comfortable time.

Then my Mother and Theresa would bring in steaming chicken soup with fluffy yellow matzah balls, and roast chicken. And when my Mum finally sat down at the table she would say to us all, with a contented smile on her face, "I feel like the last slave that has come out of Egypt."

I would always have something new to wear at

Passover, perhaps a new dress or coat, or new shoes, or if my Dad was out of work and we couldn't afford those things there would be some new socks or a new hair ribbon.

Yes, Seder nights had always been special before the war. But this year everything was mixed up. My Dad was away and Theresa was working in a munitions factory. My aunts and their families couldn't come because of the blackout. So there was only my Mum, Uncle Yudi and me. My Mum decided we would have to go somewhere else for the Seders—across the street to the Greenbergs who lived in the basement of the building. Their two sons, Alfie and Joey, were in the army, and their daughter Rosie, who was as old as I, was away in the country but would be coming home for the holiday. I'll try and get her to stay home, I thought.

Usually I hated going to the Greenbergs. Mr. Greenberg was a fat little tailor who thought he knew everything, and his wife was a pale, skinny woman with a great big pimple at the side of her nose. She seemed to be so scared of him all the time.

When I first came home from evacuation, my Mum sent me over to see them, just to be friendly, I suppose.

"What'r'ya doing home, Kitty?" Mr. Greenberg had said. "Making your mother worry again with your father away? My Rosie wouldn't do that to us now, Annie, would she?" And he looked at his wife, who nodded her head.

"My sons are in the army," he went on, "and we want

145

Rosie to be safe. She wouldn't upset her mother as you're doing. Why don't you go back?"

That was one of the reasons I didn't want to go over there. Also, Theresa had been going out with Alfie, but because Theresa's parents had been divorced Mr. Greenberg thought Theresa was no good. Or that's what he said, with a funny look on his face. And so Theresa and Alfie didn't go out any more.

The only good thing about going to Seder there was that Rosie would have to read part of the service as she was one month younger than I and Mr. Greenberg wouldn't be able to find fault with me. Mr. Greenberg's workshop was in his flat at one end of the main room and the other end was used as a living room. There were about six dirty steps going down to the flat, usually with cigarette butts in the corners, or banana or orange peel. The horrible smell of the cooking mixed with the smell of pressing made me sick. Mr. Greenberg made men's suits and every time I went down there he would be pressing jackets, smearing the lapels with a large bar of wet brown tailors' soap, and then covering the jacket with a damp cloth to iron it. A horrid smell would rise from this and, mixed with the smell of Mrs. Greenberg's cooking—usually cabbage or onions—my stomach would turn over and I would want to run out. I hated their place, but my mother said we had to go. The Greenbergs would be insulted if we didn't accept their invitation.

Still, if Rosie was there, we would have fun. She and I used to laugh together a lot before the war. But we had been evacuated to different places. Rosie had gone away with her mother at first and then her Mum had come back to help her Dad in the workshop, felling the jackets and pants, and Rosie had stayed in the country.

I was sure that Mr. Greenberg's Seder couldn't be as nice as ours, and I was sure that Mrs. Greenberg's table couldn't be as beautiful as ours. And I was right. It wasn't our house and it wasn't our way, and the smell was still there even though the machines were not running, and the pressing irons were not on the fire.

Rosie ran over to our house as soon as she got home.

"Kitty, you've got some nerve coming home without telling your Mum," she said. "My Dad would have killed me. You're lucky your Dad's away."

"My Mum tried to kill me, Rosie, but I let her have it," I smirked. "I don't think she believed what I told her. But I promised her I would make her proud of me, and that was all she wanted to hear. Why don't you try it, Rosie, and we could have a good time here? There are no bombs, nothing. This is a phony war. And Toynbee is having classes after Pesach and you could go there, too."

"Oh no," Rosie said. "My Dad would give me the strap if I asked him, let alone do it."

"Does he still take off his belt to you, Rosie?"

"Oh yes! He once tried it on Alfie, but Alfie hit him back. Thank goodness the boys are away. I'm a girl, so he thinks he can do what he likes to me. My Mum's dead scared of him. But we'll have a good time while I'm here, Kitty, and I'll stay out of his way."

"You'd better learn your Hebrew for the Seder," I said. "You're younger than me, so you have to do the Four Questions you know. And don't let him make a row at the table, Rosie, because then Uncle Yudi will poke his nose in and you know what that will mean. Let's have peace for the holiday even if it's just in the house, my Mum always says."

And so it was. The Seder was peaceful, but what a difference from ours! Mrs. Greenberg's cloth was flowered and not snowy white, and it was frayed in the corners, and the candlesticks still had some wax on them from the last time she had used them. Mr. Greenberg read through the service in Hebrew, but without asking anybody any questions, until Rosie said, "Dad, it's our turn now." He didn't seem to want to stop hearing his own voice.

"Kitty, you read, then," he said.

"No, Mr. Greenberg. I'm not the youngest. Rosie is."

"She seems much older than you," he said. "Doesn't have her own way though."

"Yes, Daddy, I am younger than Kitty."

So Rosie read her portion, faltering once or twice, her voice trembling, until she was finished. Then Mr. Greenberg went on as before with the service. Mrs. Greenberg's matzah balls were grey and small and hard as bullets. As Rosie tried to cut hers, it nearly plopped out of the bowl. The chicken soup had bits of vegetables floating on the top. Not like our clear chicken, with big yellow fluffy matzah balls and whole carrots. The chicken was overdone. But Mrs. Greenberg did make good strudel. I hoped that Mr. Greenberg hadn't used those dirty irons to press the dough to make it so thin, I thought, and giggled to myself.

After the meal we sang a lot, and that was nice. Mr. Greenberg kept on burping because of all the food he had eaten. I turned my head the other way every time it happened, but Uncle Yudi would say, "'Scuse me, Mr. Greenberg!" and Rosie would try not to laugh.

We got through it somehow. But my mind was only on the day after Easter Monday and the adventures I would have at Toynbee Hall. Even if school wouldn't be good there was always the door marked 'Seventh North Stepney Guides.' And what was behind the stage door?

26

School and After School

FINALLY the morning of classes arrived, and I was very excited. I was hoping there might be someone I knew in the class, but if not it wouldn't matter. I was sure I would make friends. The Warden hadn't told my Mum or me if there would all be girls, or boys and girls in the class, but that didn't matter.

The classroom was in the modern part of Toynbee, up on the first floor. I hurried up the stairs with my schoolbooks in my satchel. I heard giggling at the top of the stairs, and suddenly someone yelled down, "Blimey, it's Kitty Simmonds! Am I glad to see you!"

It was Esther Levy. She lived at the other end of my street and had been evacuated with her mother. I didn't even know that she had come back from evacuation. Her Mum had come back to help her Dad in his workshop, she said, just like Rosie's mother, and Esther had come back with her.

"Kitty," she said, "I'm so glad you're here! Thought I wouldn't know anyone." She gave my arm a big squeeze. We weren't such good friends before, but at least we each knew someone now. We walked arm in arm into the classroom.

It was a large room, with windows all down one side and a blackboard against one wall, but instead of desks there was a long table with chairs around it, and a teacher's desk in front of the blackboard. Four big girls were standing in the corner talking and giggling. They stopped when we came in.

"Are we in the right class?" I asked.

"I think this is the only class," one of the girls said. She had long, curly black hair hiding a very skinny face. She seemed friendly enough.

Esther and I just stood around. There were no boys in the class and I was glad of that. I didn't want to be stared at. I wore glasses, and Theresa always said that boys never made passes at girls who wore glasses. Perhaps they went in the afternoon, as we were going only in the morning, or perhaps they were all scaredy cats and had stayed in the country.

Then one of the girls suddenly whispered, "Shush, he's here." A young man who looked about as old as Theresa's boyfriend walked up to the desk in front of the blackboard. He was tall, with glasses, and said his name was Mr. Thompson, and that he would be our teacher for the next few weeks. I wondered why he wasn't in the army, and really wanted to ask him. Instead, he told us. He said that he was a "conscientious objector" which meant that he didn't believe in fighting. Instead, he said, teaching was the work that he was doing for the war effort. I didn't understand this because if a country is at war and other young men are fighting, he should fight, too. I didn't think it was very fair that he should be here. But then, if not, who would be teaching us?

My thoughts were interrupted by the sound of Mr. Thompson's voice.

"It's your turn, Miss, the girl with the glasses. Will you tell us who you are and if you've been in the country?"

I felt the blood rush to my face.

"Kitty Simmonds, sir! I've just come from Bishop Stortford."

Esther gave me a nudge.

"And I've brought my books. Here they are!"

"Good," he said. "We'll look at them later and test what level you're at."

I had been daydreaming. And the first thing I had been asked by the teacher I had messed up. I had to pay attention . . . and calm down.

I listened to the others. There were four of them:

151

Rita, Hetty, Stella and Peggy. They were all about three years older and lived on the other side of Commercial Road, almost at the docks. They hadn't been evacuated at all, and hadn't been to school since before last summer.

Mr. Thompson said he would test our skills later. He said he would put us in groups: Esther and I in one group, and the other girls in another. Was this going to be school? My hopes were going right down the drain.

Still, the girls were friendly and didn't treat us like babies.

Mr. Thompson told us that there was a lot more to Toynbee Hall besides school and that if these classes didn't work out we could take other classes here, in the evenings, like ballet and singing and music and Girl Guides.

Mr. Thompson tried very hard those next few weeks and so did we. He read stories aloud that would suit us all.

My mother was happy that I was busy. Esther and I would go to each other's houses to do our work. And there were still no bombs.

One day after school, we decided to ask the Warden about the Girl Guides room. We had wandered about Toynbee many times after class, and as I had seen the room when I was there with my Mum, I showed it to Esther. It was on the top floor in a little corner. And it was always locked. We plucked up courage and knocked on the Warden's door.

"Come in, come in," he said. We entered.

"What can I do for you, my dears? Do you like Mr.

Thompson? Is he teaching you lots and lots? Nice fellow, Thompson! Should have been in the Forces though. Still, everyone's different, and he's working out all right for you, isn't he? Thank goodness for that! Or . . . " and he looked a little startled, "have you come to complain?"

"Oh no, sir," we said together. "We want to know more about Guides."

"We saw the room," said Esther.

"And it's always locked," I said.

While we were talking, there was a knock at the door.

"Come in, come in," he said in his dark brown voice. The door opened and a very large lady was standing there. She looked quite out of breath.

"Oh, Miss Kendal," he said. "You are just the person I wanted. I was just wondering where I could get hold of you."

She was so big anybody could have got hold of her, I thought.

"You know I joined the Land Army, Mr. Richardson," she said. "Now they've sent me back to London to help with the allotments. And I'll have some spare time. So I thought I'd come round and see if there was anything I could do to help out here at Toynbee."

"Miss K., you're just the person we need. You used to run a Guide troop somewhere or other, I believe, didn't you? Well, these girls, and I think a few others in their class here at Toynbee, really need something more to do. Could you help them out? They should start to learn a bit about fire fighting, how to use a stirrup pump, and First Aid. Just in case Jerry starts to have a little fun with us. They might even use gas. But somehow, I don't think so. I think the Seventh North Stepney should get into action again. What do you think, Miss K.? If you have a minute now you could show them the Den? Kitty here says it's always locked, so now's their chance to have a look inside. But make sure the blackout curtains are drawn for tonight, won't you?"

Her face beamed. It was red and fat, and she had curly hair with little glasses perched at the tip of a small nose. She looked such a happy person, like a giant gnome.

"What a wonderful idea, Mr. Richardson! Let's talk about it, girls, before we go to the Den."

She put her arms around us, scooped us up and almost carried us out of the office into the courtyard. Then she plonked us on a bench, beaming all the time, and we began to talk about Guides.

27

Miss Kendal

OF COURSE WE WANTED to go to the Den straight away. But Miss Kendal said we should ask the other girls in the class if they wanted to join us. "After all," she said, "you can't have a Guide troop with just two girls." So we agreed that we would meet her the next day with whomever we could get to come.

We got to class early the next day and there were the others, talking and giggling in a corner as usual.

"You ask them, Esther," I whispered.

"No, you!"

"Suppose I stutter. I don't want them to laugh at me."

"Don't be daft. They won't. Go on," she said, and pushed me towards them.

"Hello," I said, and without thinking blurted it all out in one big breath, scared to stop in case I stuttered. "We're going to start a Guide troop here and are having our first meeting after school today in the Den with the captain, Miss Kendal, and she says that we need a few girls or we can't start the troop, so will you come along?"

Rita Rubin, who looked the oldest, turned to the others. "What do you think?" she asked them. They went into a huddle. Then Rita poked her head around. "Well," she said, "we have something else to do today. But you go and tell us about it and if it sounds good perhaps we'll come the next time."

"All right," I said. "But even if you are a little older she doesn't think it will make any difference."

"You tell us all about it tomorrow," Rita said again.

Just then Mr. Thompson came in and we had to start work. Never mind, I thought, Esther and I will get it going and when they hear how good it is they'll want to join.

Straight after class we rushed down to Mr. Richardson's office and there was Miss Kendal waiting and beaming.

"Hello, girls! Where are the others?"

"They said they're busy today, but that we should tell them tomorrow what we're doing," I said. "And then we're sure they'll want to join."

"You know, girls," Miss Kendal went on, "I'm told that children are slowly coming back from the country because everything is so quiet. Maybe Jerry has changed his mind about touching London. You'll see, girls, we'll make a Guide troop yet, however small for now. Now let's go up to the Den."

She took our hands and walked us through the swing doors, past the stage door, and up three flights of stairs to the corner room marked 'Seventh North Stepney Guides.' Then she unlocked the door. When she switched on the light, we could see that the blackout curtains were drawn. It was a long narrow room full of boxes with a table and a few chairs at one end, and a great big cupboard near the window at the other end. The curtains were not just plain blackouts. They were thick material with great big coloured flowers all over them. On one of the walls was a large picture of Lady Baden-Powell. Opposite was a picture of King George. The room smelled old and musty.

"This room has obviously not been used in ever such a long time," Miss Kendal said. "Now let's see what's in these boxes. I don't think we could ever have a big troop up here. It'd be fine for a dozen or so when we get this mess cleared up. But I'm sure Mr. Richardson would let us use the canteen if we have more."

We began to open the boxes. There were Guide uniforms, camping stuff, and even a great big rolled up tent. We piled the boxes on top of one another so that we could move around. Then Miss Kendal opened the big wooden cupboard. Everything inside was neat and tidy. There were badges with elves on them—she said they were Tenderfoot badges—and all kinds of ribbons for special tests we would have to pass, and chalk and small blackboards and stiff coloured paper and crepe paper. Everything was in perfect order and there was still plenty of room. Miss Kendal told us to stack the uniforms and camping stuff in the cupboard as well. Then she showed us a book called *A Handbook for Guides* with a picture of Lady Baden-Powell on the front. She gave us each a copy to take home.

"As soon as we have more girls we can start a troop," she said. "The book will give you some ideas. Meanwhile we'll meet up here Tuesdays and Thursdays to get a feel for the place and we'll start learning some First Aid even if there are only two of you."

Then she started poking through some of the boxes we hadn't opened yet.

"By Jove," she said. "Here's my Guider's hat. Thought I'd lost it. Look at it, squashed flat." She picked it up and put it on. It was squashed, and dusty besides. But she put one brim up and the other down, wrinkled her nose, and grinned. "Well, how do I look, girls? Think it makes me look a proper Captain?"

"Smashing," we said, and laughed.

"Come," she said, "let's go down now. Next time we'll look through the songbook. I'm sure there'll be some in there you know."

She switched off the light, locked the door, and we started down the stairs. The building was very quiet, but as we turned the first landing we heard someone whistling, and a young man came bounding up the stairs. He was wearing a skirt with a great wide paint brush hanging from his waist in front, the kind of brush my Dad used to whitewash the kitchen ceiling. When he saw us he stopped.

"Well! Maggie Kendal!" he said. "How good to see you. Richardson told me you were here, so I came to have a quick natter."

"Bless my soul, it's Charlie Salter," Miss Kendal exclaimed. "How good to see you."

"What are you doing back, Maggie? Dick told me you were starting a Guide troop again. How do you have the time?"

"Well, these girls need something else besides the few hours of school they're getting here. But let me introduce you." And she turned to us. "Esther Levy and Kitty Simmonds. Dr. Salter. He's Scots, and lots of fun!"

I looked at Esther. Her hand was over her mouth and I knew she was killing herself laughing but trying to be polite at the same time. But Miss Kendal and Dr. Salter were so busy talking to each other I hoped they didn't see her. I looked down trying to hide my face. And as I did I saw long skinny legs in green checked socks up to the knees above men's shoes. I couldn't believe it.

"You look very dapper, Charlie!" I heard Miss Kendal say. "But why are you all dressed up in kilt and sporan? Is there something special on today?"

"Well, I'm at London Hospital, just across the street, you know. Tonight we're putting on a show for the patients. The place is nearly empty, waiting for Jerry to attack. But the patients who are there are not very happy. So we thought we'd cheer them up with some Scottish reels, and a sword dance to show off, perhaps. There are a few of us Scots there. It will be good for the patients. Come to think of it, Maggie, I could teach your girls some Scottish dances if they'd like. And we can put on a show in the theatre downstairs for their Mums and any Dads that are around. You remember we did Hiawatha once? Why don't we do it again with these girls?"

Then he looked at Esther.

"By Jove," he exclaimed. "You'd make a perfect Hiawatha. Just the right face!"

I looked at Esther. Hiawatha was an Indian, I remembered. And Esther is dark skinned. But she's a Jewish girl from my street. She doesn't look like an Indian to me. Then he looked at me. He pulled his hand through his curly red hair and seemed to be thinking.

"Now Kitty," he said. "Don't know about you. You're too fair. You won't be any good for Minnie Ha Ha."

He crinkled up his forehead. "Oh, I know. We could cover your hair and charcoal your face. Can you sing?"

"Oh yes," I said, "I love to sing."

"All right then. Perhaps you can be Chibiabos, the musician. I think he came from some mixed clan or other so colour doesn't matter so much."

"Who's that?" I said, giggling at the funny sounding name.

"He's the musician who sings in the forest. Beautiful love songs." And he began to sing: "'On away awake beloved . . . .' And you'll do your Scottish dancing, prancing all over the stage. And Miss Kendal will make a speech. And everyone will clap."

"Oh enough, Charlie! You are a scream," said Miss Kendal. "First we have to teach them other things, like First Aid. Never know when Jerry will strike. Be Prepared—that's the Girl Guides' motto, eh girls?"

"Yes, and how to use stirrup pumps," he burst in. "Have to know how to put out the incendiary bombs they keep talking about. Yes, so much to do! I hope we can get it all in before Jerry comes. Anyway, Maggie, have to get to the London for a rehearsal. Bye, Maggie. 'Tra girls." And he bounded down the stairs, kilt flying.

Miss Kendal looked at us.

"Well," she said. "What do you think of him? He'll be a marvellous help to us. We've got lots to look forward to."

She grinned. Esther and I looked at each other. Yes, there was lots to look forward to.

28
Finale

MISS KENDAL did as she had promised, and Girl Guides began.

There was still no war in London. The phony war was still going . . . the blackout, but no bombs, nothing. London was quiet, and the announcer on the wireless said that children had begun to come back from evacuation. I was glad.

One Sunday morning I was just running up the street to Esther Levy's house, when Rosie Greenberg rushed over to meet me.

"Kitty, Kitty," she said, "I'm home. I made my Mum bring me back as nothing is happening here. The war will soon be over. Even though Joey and Alfie are in France, it's happening there and not here. So I'm home for good, my Mum says. Course my Dad blamed you and had a big row with my Mum. But she's still letting me stay. So he's not talking to her. I'm so happy to be here and not with all those cows. Where are you going, Kitty?"

So I told her about Esther Levy, and the school in Toynbee Hall, and the Guides we hoped to have. She was so excited.

"Can I come with you, now?" she asked.

"Oh, yes! Esther will be really glad to have you in Guides. We haven't got many people yet, but perhaps Ada Skaradick and Prisci Maransky will come back, too, and they'll join."

Esther was really glad to see Rosie. She knew her from the street, but not well. We played in her yard and showed Rosie the book Miss Kendal had given us, and tried to do the knots that were shown in the book with a bit of rope Esther had got from her Dad.

The next day Rosie joined Toynbee with us. Poor Mr. Thompson! Every few days a new person showed up in his class. But we were happy.

One Tuesday the older girls decided they would come to the Den. Miss Kendal was pleased about that and the Guide troop gradually grew. We divided into patrols, and of course the older girls were the leaders, but it didn't matter to us. We all did the same things.

Miss Kendal asked Mr. Radford, the fire watcher at Toynbee, to teach us how to use the stirrup pump to put out incendiary bombs. One Sunday morning we all met in the courtyard for our first lesson.

"Now lie flat on your stomach, girls, and keep your head down," Mr. Radford said. "Hold the pump up over your head and point it towards the incendiary bomb."

He had put a football into a pail pretending it was an incendiary and we had to squirt the water on it, without getting the water in our faces. It was hard, and most of us got soaked.

"With practice, girls, you'll do it, I'm sure. But keep those faces right down. Don't want any sparks to fly at you. Next week I'll make a real fire in that pail, and get some tin hats for you to put on. That'll be real practice. And I'll talk about gas 'cause Jerry might even use that.

We'll talk about tear gas, and mustard gas, and lewisite, which smells just like geraniums. In front of the office there's a great big pot of red geraniums. Go and smell them. That's what lewisite smells like. But we'll talk about it next week. See you then."

Would we ever have to use this practice? And would we ever have to smell that gas? I hoped not. It was a bit scary. But we were all so sure no bombs would come. It was only the grown ups that thought they would.

"When will we learn First Aid?" Rosie asked Miss Kendal one day. "My Joey writes that we'll need it in London if the bombs come."

"How would he know?" I said. "He's in France. It's different from here."

"He knows," Rosie said. "He's a soldier. Perhaps a Jerry told him." And we all laughed.

But at the next Guide meeting Miss Kendal announced that someone from the Red Cross would be coming to give us a few lessons in First Aid.

I ran home from Guides that night, so excited.

"Mum," I said, "we're going to learn First Aid, and if anything happens we'll be able to help the wounded."

My mother's face turned white. I thought she was going to faint.

"If any bombs come, Kitty," she said, "you won't be staying here to do your First Aid. I should never have let you stay at home."

She turned her head away. I thought she was going to cry.

But we did do First Aid, and there were still no bombs. We learned how to lift someone onto a stretcher with help, how to do a tourniquet to stop bleeding, how to tie a bandage properly, and even how to make a splint from a piece of wood. And we all took turns being wounded. When it was Rosie's turn to be lifted onto the stretcher, she was so heavy and was giggling so much that the stretcher turned upside down and she fell flat on her face. Did we laugh!

But after a while we got the idea of it. It was fun! Esther, Rosie and I worked together without even having a row. We had become good friends.

The weeks went by and our Guide company grew. We were not only learning firefighting and First Aid but even trying for our Cook's badge. Mr. Richardson let us use the canteen to make scrambled eggs, and bangers 'n mash. I had watched my Mum making bangers 'n mash— lovely mashed potatoes with fried onions, and sausages which burst with a bang as they sizzled in the pan. What a lark it was cutting up those onions. My Mum had never let me help in the kitchen, but I used to watch her when I was reading on the sofa.

"Stop crying," Esther said to me as I was cutting up the onions. She was killing herself laughing.

"I'm not crying, silly! It's these onions. You have a go and you'll see." And she cried too.

With the bangers 'n mash, and the scrambled eggs, we all passed our Cook's badge, which we sewed on the sleeve of our uniform. That was our first badge.

When I got home with it Uncle Yudi did make me laugh.

"Now we can send your Mum on evacuation and you can stay 'ere and look after me and the cat," he said. He grinned that great big grin that seemed to stretch from one ear to the other, his cigarette sticking out of the corner of his mouth.

One day at the beginning of June Mrs. Greenberg came running into the shop.

"Mrs. Simmonds! Yudi!" she called. "Did you hear what they just said on the wireless? The army has pulled back to Dunkirk, and they've sent over our boats to bring them back. My Alfie and Joey are in France. They said there are terrible losses." And she burst into tears.

"Come into the kitchen, Mrs. Greenberg," my Mum said.

"I'll make you a cuppa," said Uncle Yudi.

I asked where Rosie was. "She's with her Dad. Go over and keep her company, Kitty," Mrs. Greenberg sobbed.

"They'll be all right," my Mum said. "You'll see."

"England's got a strong army," Uncle Yudi said. "We won't take any guff from those bloody Germans. Pity I'm not younger. Would have gone over and 'elped 'em myself. But they don't want old ones like me. Forty-five's too old for 'em."

"Hurry up, Kitty," my Mum said. "Go over to Rosie already."

But it wasn't all right. Joey came home on leave after a few weeks. But they still didn't know where Alfie was.

The pullback had been such a muddle. Finally, the War Office let Rosie's Dad know that Alfie was found badly wounded and was in a hospital in Exeter.

Now the war was getting close and people were sure England would be invaded soon.

Everyone who came into the shop was talking about the air raids on the south coast. The Germans were trying to bomb air force bases and we could see fighter planes overhead. Then the air raid siren would go and we would run into the street shelters. They were horrible, always smelling of cats. I told my Mum I wouldn't go, even in the daytime, when I was at home. Of course, at Toynbee we had to run into the cellar under the stage door when the siren went. Mr. Thompson would hustle us out of class, making sure we had our gas masks with us. But the alarm didn't go on for very long, and there were no bombs. We didn't see many fights in the air at first, only white streaks from the planes as they flew away. Sometimes the siren would go at night and my Mum would get into a panic.

"Come on Kitty! We must run to the shelter."

I would turn over and go to sleep. Then Theresa would yell up the stairs, "It's all right, Auntie Passie. Nothing's going to happen. The planes are just going over."

But my Mum took no notice, and dragged me out of bed.

"Come on, Theresa," she'd say. "Where's Yudi?"

"He's not going and I'm not going," Theresa said.

"And I'm not either," I said.

But she still dragged me, and sometimes by the time she got me down the stairs and out the door ready to run to the crypt of the church around the corner the All Clear would go, and Theresa would laugh.

"I told you, Auntie Passie," she'd say. And we would hear Uncle Yudi snoring away upstairs.

This went on for weeks, right through the summer.

One Saturday afternoon at the beginning of September, my Mum asked me to walk with her to Wickham's. It was a big shop at the bottom of Mile End Road, a long walk from our house. But the weather was good, warm and sunny, and Wickham's had a big sale. My Mum never went shopping for food on Saturdays, but she liked to go to the shops and look around. Saturdays was the day she relaxed, she said. No cooking, no cleaning. Just enjoy the Sabbath in her way.

Sometimes she would see a dress either for me or for herself and would put a deposit on it and go the next week to buy it. I liked going with her. It was a day she didn't nag me and I felt warm and comfy beside her. But I did feel so lonely without my Dad, even though Theresa and Uncle Yudi were in the house. I wished my Dad would hurry up and come home. Then my Mum wouldn't be so worried about me all the time, and every day would be like Saturday.

It was a long walk to Wickham's. We didn't hurry to get there. The stalls were out along the Mile End Road, selling underwear, or pots and pans. We stopped here and there to have a look. But that day we didn't buy anything except an ice lolly from the Wall's man outside Wickham's.

"Don't spill it on your good dress," my Mum said. I felt the nagging was going to start again.

"We'd better hurry home now. It's a long way and Yudi will be wanting supper."

It was about five o'clock and we were passing Lyons' tea shop, opposite the London Hospital by Whitechapel Station. Suddenly the air raid siren wailed. My Mum grabbed my hand and we both looked up in the sky. This time we didn't see any fighter planes, as we had during the summer. The sky was clear. But suddenly we heard a tremendous whoosh and then a crash.

Everything seemed to stop on the street. Then air raid wardens began running and blowing their whistles.

"Everyone take cover," a warden shouted. He pushed my Mum, who was standing like a statue. She seemed to be stuck to the ground.

"C'mon Mum," I said. She wouldn't move.

"Quick lady," he said. "Into the station with that child." And he pushed us through the tube station's open doors. We both ran down the stairs, people pushing us along. The station wasn't very deep and so we could hear the bombs coming down, with quiet times in between, and everyone, I thought, holding their breath.

I wanted to go up and look, but I knew my Mum wouldn't let me.

"I'll just be a second, Mum," I said. "I'm just going to

have a look." And I darted towards the stairs.

"Get back, girl," a warden shouted at me. He grabbed my arm and pushed me back.

"Thanks, Guv," my Mum said, grabbing onto me.

Everyone was hardly breathing. Then there was another bang and another. The lights in the station flickered. We trembled. Then there was a great silence.

"I hope Yudi and Theresa are all right," I heard my Mum mumbling. "I hope they don't hit our house."

Then a warden came down.

"Was the hospital hit?" somebody asked him.

"No. But all behind the hospital. They must have hit the docks. All the smoke's coming from that way."

No noise outside and no one speaking inside. We were all waiting. But instead we heard this long shrill note that we had heard so many times before. It was the All Clear. We could leave the station.

The whole thing had taken less than an hour.

When we got outside the sky was black with smoke behind the London hospital. But nothing on Whitechapel High Street was damaged.

"Quick, Kitty," my Mum said. "We must find Yudi and Theresa. I only hope they're alive."

"Mum," I said, "they said it was the docks. Our house is the other way."

"Who knows," she said. "Quick. Come." And we hurried home.

But our street and house were perfect. Uncle Yudi was drinking tea and he said that Theresa had just gone out with her boyfriend.

"What's ya so worried for, Passie?" he said. "Sit down. I'll make you a cuppa. Told ya' everything'd be all right."

When I told him we'd been pushed into Whitechapel Station, he looked at me funny.

"What bloody good is that station? It's all open at the bottom by the platform. You might as well have come 'ome. Those docks 'ave 'ad quite a bashing. The Jerrys'll probably be back tonight again to finish the job. Hitler said 'e would destroy us. But 'e won't. I think 'e'll 'ave a bloody good try, though. For your Mum's sake, you'd better go to the shelter tonight, Kitty. The crypt of All Saints is the nearest. You can run there in your nightie if you 'ave to. I'll stay 'ere with Theresa and look after the cat. So don't worry, Passie."

By the time it got dark, the siren still hadn't sounded. But when it finally did go long after we were in bed I turned over, hoping my Mum wouldn't hear it. But then I heard Uncle Yudi's voice calling from his room: "I told you so, Kitty. The Jerrys are back to finish the job."

My Mum woke up. "Where's my glasses?" she said, feeling all over the chair beside her bed for them. She must have been in such a state when she went to bed. She must have forgotten to take them off, for there they were right at the tip of her nose.

"Hurry, Kitty! Don't get dressed. Just put on your coat and let's run!"

Uncle Yudi came out of his room in his long underwear.

"Get up, girl, and go with your Mum, or she'll have a fit. You know 'ow bloomin' frightened she is for you. And it's likely going to be a bad one tonight."

He pulled me out of bed and we ran down the stairs.

"Are you coming, Yudi?" my Mum yelled.

"No, of course not," he said. "And Theresa's fast asleep. But you run." And he pushed us out the door. The siren had stopped. Already we heard the ack-ack in the distance. Then we saw Rosie and her Mum.

"Run to All Saints," Mrs. Greenberg said.

We ran around the corner and down the stairs into the crypt of the church.

It was crowded already, with everyone sitting squashed on benches with their coats over their night clothes. Mr. Belinsky even had a nightcap on. He must have forgotten to take it off in the panic of running for shelter. I wanted to laugh. Yet there I was with my Mum, both of us in our flannel nighties. We must have looked a sight to him. My Mum looked so frightened that I was glad Uncle Yudi had made me come with her.

Everyone was grumbling that they hoped this wouldn't go on all night. We heard banging outside, but not too close. Before I knew what happened, I had fallen asleep with my head resting on my Mum's lap. I didn't hear anything else until I felt someone shaking me. It was my Mum.

"It's five o'clock, Kitty," she said. "The All Clear's gone. It's time to go home."

Where was I? I didn't even remember. Then I saw

Mr. Belinsky in his nightcap and I knew where I was.

Everyone was rubbing their eyes and stretching as we left the church and went home. Nothing on the street was damaged. We saw smoke, lots of black smoke, in the sky towards the docks.

"They must have hit the docks again," my Mum said.

"I wonder when we're going to get it," I said.

"Bite your tongue, Kitty. Don't ever say that."

"Yudi, Yudi" my Mum called when we got to our house. But all we heard was a loud snore. She went up into Theresa's room and opened the door quietly. There was Theresa, sleeping peacefully as if nothing had happened.

"Tomorrow night, Mum, if the siren goes I'm staying home too," I said. "Theresa is sleeping away. She hasn't heard a thing. And Uncle Yudi is snoring away upstairs."

"We'll see about that," she said. But she cuddled me close. We went upstairs to bed.

It was hard going to school after being up half the night and not sleeping very much, but my Mum made me go. And Mr. Thompson didn't work us too hard. Thank goodness there were no air raids that day, but the next night, and for many nights after that, we had to run to the shelter, even though I fought to stay home. Every time I tried to argue with my Mum, she started screaming at me. I just had to go.

While I was at school one day a time bomb was found in All Saints and we couldn't go to the crypt any more. So we spent many more nights in the cellar of Truman's Brewery at the other end of our street. Some of the men

172

joked that they hoped it would be hit so that the beer would run like water. That did make everyone laugh.

But one night a time bomb fell on Truman's and we all had to get out quickly and run to the Fruit Exchange in Spitalfield. That was awful. The smell of the rotten vegetables and fruit made me feel sick. There was nowhere else nearby to go, my Mum said, so we had to spend nights there carrying our blankets back and forth.

Then for a few days there was a lull. No night raids—and a good night's sleep. But that Saturday evening, the siren went again. And by the time we got to the Fruit Exchange, it was full. There was no room for us. My mother started to cry.

"Let's go home, Mum" I said. "There's no noise. And I can't hear any ack-ack."

"Oh no!" she said. "It'll soon start. Come, we'll run to the tube."

Some others who couldn't get in either thought that was a good idea. So we all ran, mothers dragging their children and carting their blankets, to Liverpool Street Station. And still it was quiet even though the siren had sounded.

The station was crowded, too, with the usual hustle and bustle of soldiers coming and going. The tube platform was full too, with people lying on their blankets. There was no room for us. The next stop was the Bank. That was full, too.

"What are we going to do?" my Mum said, tears streaming down her face.

"Try the next one lady," a man in the crowd said. We did, and at St. Paul's Station there was space, just for my Mum and me.

But each night I hated it more and more.

Then one night, just before dusk when I knew my Mum would begin to nag, I made up my mind not to go to the tube any more. I was sick to death of running every night, sick to death of sleeping on the hard cold platform with the trains going by, and everyone staring, and the horrible smells of sweaty people and smelly blankets.

Theresa and Uncle Yudi still wouldn't go. They still slept in the house—Uncle Yudi after his firewatching and Theresa after her shift in the munitions factory. Or so they told us.

So why should I have to go? Theresa and Uncle Yudi said again and again that if your number was on a bomb it would hit you, so why run? But my Mum didn't think that way and so every night she nagged and every night we ran.

That night I was upstairs in the front room fiddling on the piano, dreaming, and looking at what was left of my parents' wedding cake, sitting in its glass case on top of the piano. Mum had kept a layer all these years. It sat on three little pillars made of icing sugar, the sugar bride and groom decorating the top. The groom even wore a little black top hat.

I wondered what my Mum had been like as a bride and my Dad as a groom. To me they seemed so old. Whenever I looked at the figures I always made up stories about how they had met, because they had never told me about that. Right now I wanted to stay with that bride and groom. I didn't want to get mixed up with the hustle and bustle of sirens and bombs and shelters.

Suddenly, my mother's voice broke through. "Hurry, Kitty. Hurry and get dressed. It's time to go. Come on. Let's go."

But that night, I didn't want to go, and I wouldn't go. I just kept on playing the piano.

"I'm not calling you again, Kitty," she yelled up the stairs. "You come right down. Now!"

I slammed down the piano lid, nearly catching my fingers, slammed the door of the front room, and clumped down the stairs . . . in my underwear.

She was at the cooker frying salmon rissoles to take for our supper at the tube. She turned when she heard me.

"Still not dressed! Do you want us to be killed?"

"No, Mum. But I'm not going tonight." I stood in a corner watching her. Her hands were trembling, and the oil in the pan was splattering. "Like Theresa and Uncle Yudi said . . . ."

"Theresa and Uncle Yudi are stupid," she said. "Your Dad is away and I promised him I'd keep you safe. So you'll come, and you'll come now. Get upstairs and get dressed!"

I started to cry and, in a temper, ripped my clothes. My mother kept on cooking the supper, her hands still trembling.

Suddenly a salmon rissole came flying through the

175

air, landing with a dull thud on the wall just above my head. It missed me by inches, the grease splashing all over the wallpaper behind me.

She had lost control. She had never done this before. Tears welled in her eyes.

I crumpled to the ground, sobbing. "I don't want to go, Mummy. Please don't make me."

We were both exhausted, but she took my hand, put her arm around me and, tears streaming down both our faces, took me up to my room and helped me get dressed.

"Come on, Dolly," she said, trying to be nice to me now.

My poor Mum, I thought. She knew she had gone too far.

We started out. I couldn't walk as fast as she, and I didn't want to. She pulled and dragged me along the many streets towards the tube.

Dusk was already closing in and we were still a turning or two before Liverpool Street when the terrible wailing of the siren began.

My Mum stopped dead. She pulled at her hair. "I told you we should have started out before," she screamed. "They're starting early tonight." And she didn't move.

Then the banging began . . . the ack-ack of the guns, and the whistle of bombs. Around us everyone was running like mad.

I threw my arms around her. "C'mon Mum. We have to run." But she wouldn't move.

"Help! Help!" I yelled.

A warden came running out of the dark.

"What's the matter girl? Run!"

"My Mum won't move. And I can't leave her!"

"C'mon, lady!" And he pushed her.

"I promised Sam I would look after her. And now she's going to get killed!"

"Stop it, stop it, lady! Run!"

He slapped my Mum's face. I put my arm around her and held her tight.

"Come on, Mum! Let's run! I'll be all right."

I pulled her and dragged her the rest of the way to Liverpool Street Station.

By the time we got to our places at St. Paul's, I knew that one thing was for sure: from now on until the end of the bombing, this platform would be our bed.

So it's down, down in the Underground
To shelter from the noise and blast
Nice girls there, everywhere,
And you find as you go down Leicester Square,
Cocoa, sausage rolls, hot meat pies
A cup of tea, a piece of cake or p'r'aps a bag of fries
So it's down, down in the Underground
And oh what wonderful sights you'll see
Beneath the bunk of Lady Lottie,
You'll find my one-eyed Scottie
In the Underground in good old London town.

The Great Fire of London

WE WERE ALWAYS taught at school that the Great Fire of London was in 1666, but for me the Great Fire of London was on the 10th of May 1941, when the Luftwaffe tried to destroy the whole City of London.

What a terrible night that was, the worst night of the Blitz.

Dusk was closing in. My mother and I were a turning or two from Liverpool Street Station when we heard the terrible wailing of the air raid siren, the banging of the ack-ack guns, and the whistling of bombs. Around us everyone was running like mad to get to the station. When I finally got Mum on the train, people were saying it was going to be a bad night. And when we finally arrived at St. Paul's tube station, even on the platform so deep underground, we could hear loud banging above us.

Some of the old men went to the top of the escalator to see what was going on and came down with grim reports.

"That there milk bar across the road had a direct hit. You should see. Twisted metal and rubble. Some people were killed," they said. "Ambulances, with sirens blaring, were taking the injured to Barts Hospital up the street. We wanted to help but the wardens made us go back downstairs. 'Don't want to have to cart you bloody lot off on stretchers to Barts as well,' they told us."

And then all the lights went out. It was awful. But there must have been some emergency equipment as the porters had the lights on in a short time. It was all so scary. I clung to Mummy and she to me.

We slept very little on the cold, hard platform that night. Everyone was grumbling, yawning, and trying to sleep. And then one old man near us started to sing. "Maybe he's having a nightmare," Mummy whispered.

I thought it was Mr. Marks, the herring man from Petticoat Lane, until I heard a woman say, "Izzy, stop your snoring," so it couldn't have been him. My Mum said that Mr. Marks' name was Abe.

Then another voice, not singing, but yelling.

"That's that crazy bagel woman at the corner of Old Montague Street," Mummy said. "Wonder she's not trying to sell her bagels down here." Someone told her to shut up.

It was quiet on the platform for a little while. Then the banging up above started again and another voice began to sing. It sounded like a foreign voice to me.

"Who's that, Mum?"

"Don't know. There's so many different kinds of people down here. The theatres and nightclubs in the West End are open, even in the raids. It must be some actor or toff who got stuck on the platform who's singing now."

Slowly some people joined in: "*So it's down, down in the Underground . . . .*" I suppose they wanted to drown out the noise of the banging above.

It was a long time before we got to sleep again. It seemed like as soon as we fell asleep we heard the porters shouting, "No trains running this morning, ducks. You'll have to walk home."

All of a sudden, everything was in a turmoil. Everyone was tired and grumpy. Like us, most people lived a long way from St. Paul's, and some people wanted to stay on the platform all day in case of more raids. But the porters wouldn't let them and tried to make us line up to get on the escalator. But of course, the escalator was shut down and everyone would have to walk up the million stairs to get to the top. People were pushing and shoving, trying to get up the stairs to find out what had happened to their homes. As we waited our turn, Mummy worried out loud, over and over again, "I hope Theresa and Yudi are all right."

Then some woman tripped and the person behind

her fell over her. "Take it easy there," a porter shouted to the crowd. "Remember what happened at Bethnal Green tube a few nights ago with the pushing and shoving. Don't want any more people killed." That calmed everybody down some. Slowly, slowly, we reached the top and the exit.

Thank goodness by this time we didn't have to take our blankets home. Someone had organized a storage place on the platform for them. We paid for a ticket and collected them the next night.

The sight at the exit was more than we could bear. The milk bar was a mess and the acrid smell of smoke and soot nearly choked us. Small fires were burning all around. All my Mum could say was, again, "I hope Theresa and Yudi are all right. They're so cocky. Maybe they'll come with us now . . . if they're still alive."

We walked to the corner of St. Paul's churchyard. Its wall had been smashed by the blast but by some miracle the church dome was still in place.

We walked down Cheapside. Fires were burning everywhere from incendiary bombs. Firemen were stretched flat out with stirrup pumps trying to put out the fires, while air raid wardens were directing people trekking home from all this. I had learned how to use a stirrup pump at Girl Guides, but of course neither the air raid wardens nor Mummy would let me help.

Many of the buildings were badly damaged—not just from the incendiaries but from bombs also—in the actual City of London where the government buildings, shipping offices, the Royal Mint, the Mansion House where the Lord Mayor of London had his headquarters, and most of the newspaper offices, were. This was what the Luftwaffe obviously wanted to destroy that night. They had a good try.

Afterwards people said how stupid the Germans had been to have chosen a Saturday night when the whole City of London was closed down anyway. "But after all," Mummy said, "there are caretakers there and firewatchers and they could get killed."

Through Leadenhall Street we walked to Aldgate pump, which was at the end of the old City of London. More fires. More rubble. Staircases with housefronts blown away. It took such a long time and we were so tired. When we came to Osborne Street we found it completely cordoned off. The Victoria Wine Company had had a direct hit and we were told that when the firemen went in to control the flames the alcohol fumes made them drunk and they had to be carried out on stretchers.

Finally we got to the top of our street. It didn't look too bad, just a few broken windows, but there were plenty of those even before. When we came to our block, there was devastation. In the midst of it, Uncle Yudi and Theresa were trying to sort out the mess around our house. "Thank God, you're all right," Mummy cried, and she rushed over to them, tears streaming down her face.

There had been a bomb behind our house and the blast had blown everything of ours out onto the street. Daddy's jacket, which had been hanging on the door of the front room near the piano, had been blasted through the window. Still on its hanger, it was stuck on the outside wall of the house riddled with holes. Sheet music, which I had left on the piano, lay scattered in the road.

"Theresa, Yudi, thank God you're alive," my Mum cried. "Were you in the house?"

"Give over, Auntie Passie, would I be here if I was in the house?" said Theresa. "I went to my Dad's, and stayed there."

"And you, Yudi?" she asked.

"Where do you think, Pas? In the Frying Pan pub. It's at the corner of Thrawl Street, not far from the wine company. Was that a mess! Knew a few of the firemen. They always wanted to get drunk, but I don't think like that." And his usual big grin turned to a sad smile.

"Is your father's milk shed all right, Theresa?" asked my Mum. "We'd better go and look."

His shed was around the corner. And it, too, had been blasted. The milk churns were all on their sides and milk was running into the gutter.

"What a bloody mess!" was Uncle Yudi's comment. "Dave will be happy he won't have to work for a couple of days."

My two uncles were not good friends. Uncle Davey, Theresa's father, was a hard worker, but Uncle Yudi loved the horses best and let the milk shop go down.

Theresa gave him a dirty look. "Perhaps you'll have to help him clean up now, Uncle Yudi," she said.

I didn't care so much about Uncle Davey's milk shed. I cared much more about my house. Where would we live now? Would we have to sleep in that dirty and noisy tube station forever?

And then I saw my bride and groom that had been on top of the piano before we had left the house. They were lying together beside the now broken wedding cake, intact, side by side, on their pillars. I picked them up and cuddled them. My fantasy friends hadn't died.

"Come, Kitty. Help clean up," I heard Mummy say. But for the time being she left me cuddling my bride and groom. If we had stayed in the house, like my bride and groom, would we have been saved, too, I wondered?

LATER AN AIR RAID warden took us to the closest rest centre, which was in my old infant school. We were not allowed to go back into our house as it was too dangerous and had to be boarded up, especially, as my Mum told me later, since people had been looting things from bombed-out houses.

Our neighbours, the Greenbergs, had asked us to stay with them. My Mum thought that was very nice of them as their basement flat was very small. But their son was killed a few weeks before in the army and they were in a terrible state. It would be better, Mum said, to stay in the rest centre.

They gave us each a camp bed and a blanket, so at least we would not have to sleep on the ground as we did in the tube platform. It was comfy enough, but the place still reeked from smelly people and smelly blankets, just like the tube.

Volunteers, usually from the posh parts of London, would come down to help in the rest centres. Canteens were organized there and during a raid, firemen, who were completely exhausted, faces black from soot and sweat, would come in for a sandwich or two and usually a hot cup of strong tea to keep them going the rest of the night. But mainly the rest centre was used for people who had been bombed out of their homes and were waiting, sometimes for months, for a new house to stay in. And sometimes, yes, the rest centre itself was bombed. They were mainly in schools until large numbers of children returned from evacuation. Then rest centres were difficult to find.

We stayed there for a few weeks, and it was horrible: smelly and noisy. Finally the Council found us a place a few streets from the shop and we all moved in. Theresa decided to stay with her Dad and Uncle Yudi, of course, came with us. It was not a very nice house. The floors sloped but my Mum said it was better than nothing and we stayed there for a while. Then my Mum saw a little house across the street. The people had moved to the country and so we moved in and stayed there for a long time.

The raids were still on but somehow nothing happened to that house. Uncle Yudi still had his untidy room on the main floor and we lived mainly in the kitchen at the back of the house, with the little front parlour only used for visitors. Somehow our piano survived all the moves and the blast, so it was there, too. For the first time I had a room of my own upstairs and my Mum in the room next to it; the spare room, as my Mum called it, would be where my Dad did his woodworking when he came home, and he repaired our shoes. I can still see him putting our shoes on the last, nails in his mouth, hammer in his hand, nailing soles and heels for us.

WE DIDN'T REALIZE that that Saturday, the 10th of May, was to be the worst of the Big Blitz raids, and so every night for a little while we went to the tube, even though the raids continued on and off during the day and night. But then there was a lull, and that was wonderful: no running every night and I could sleep in my own room, snuggling under the covers. But that lull was too good to last, as my Mum said, and in November 1942 another Little Blitz, as everyone called it, went on until the next summer and once again we ran to the tube every night. By that time two-tiered bunks had been put up on the platform so we didn't have to sleep on the cold, hard floor anymore. And then another lull.

Everyone was wondering when this bloody war would end and we wanted so much for my Dad to come home. Finally, just before Pesach, he did come home, looking so skinny. My Mum's first words were: "Sam, how did you get so thin? Didn't you eat anything, even with the parcels I sent you?"

"Passie, I had your parcels, tried to share them with

the men, but they were greedy and took the best part, and at night they would catch a rabbit, skin it and stew it in a pail over the fire. Sometimes they used that pail for their washing. How could I eat from it? I couldn't touch it, not kosher first of all, and seeing the little animal running around in the fields all day, I couldn't, Passie. All I need now is a good cup of tea and some of your chicken soup with knaidlech. That'll do the trick."

I cuddled him and could feel his bones. Poor Daddy.

"It's all right, Sam," Mum said. "I'll fatten you up."

My dear Dad was a very quiet man. He seldom argued, and so I could imagine all those heavy men taking the best from his parcels and he not fighting back. I loved him so much.

But as much food as Mum gave him, he didn't get any fatter. And we worried plenty about him.

While we were talking, Uncle Yudi walked in.

"Sam! Glad you're home. Good to see you! But you look bloody thin. What happened?"

"There's a war on, Yudi, didn't you know? We didn't get much good food while we were building those army huts."

Although my Dad and Uncle Yudi hadn't spoken much before Dad went away, they sounded friendly enough now.

ANOTHER ROUND of bombs came in June 1944, but these were very different.

By that time I had left school, as much as there was of

it. Toynbee Hall was my school but classes closed when teachers were sent on war work, and so I found a job as office girl with the London County Council at County Hall on the end of Westminster Bridge.

The raids continued, but now mostly in the daytime. One day the siren went and we heard the roar of a plane overhead. Some people rushed down to the shelter. Others, me included, lay flat on the hallway floor waiting for the bomb to explode, but nothing happened. There was a terrible silence for a few seconds and then . . . *bang*! The buildings shook around us and we heard glass shattering.

This was one of the first doodle bugs, or V1s, that hit London. It was horrible. These V1s were catapulted straight up and glided with no sound to their target, then fell. After that, everyone held their breath until they heard the bang. The bomb that we heard that day had fallen directly on a bus full of people outside Waterloo Station, which was at the back of County Hall. We ran out of the office to help. I straggled behind and my boss made me go back, but I saw the bus, completely destroyed and human limbs scattered around. I felt sick.

Of course I was sent home, being the youngest in the office, and my Mum was so worried about me. Soon after my body began to itch, and I came out in square hives, which Mummy had never seen before, and she rushed me to the London Hospital nearby. Ugh. They injected me with something and slowly slowly the hives and the itch disappeared. The doctor said it was the shock of all that had happened. Mummy said it could have been worse and that God was looking after us. But all those people on the bus! I had nightmares for a long time after that.

After the doodlebugs, the Germans, knowing they couldn't win this war, made one more try to destroy us with the V2 rocket, and with this one there was no warning. One of the last V2s fell a few blocks from our house. We were in the kitchen at the time and suddenly heard a terrible bang. Our curtains fell down and some of the windows smashed. We ran into the street and saw that the rocket had fallen on a block of flats up the street, across from a school. Thank goodness the school was empty but many people in the flats were killed, including my friend Phyllis Veltman. She was a lovely girl with long black curly hair and always a smile on her face. What a sad day for all of us.

But soon after, V-E (Victory in Europe) Day came.

By that time I had joined a youth club, and after every raid we would go to one another's houses to help clean up. When that last rocket struck the boys were ready, boarding up our windows and putting the curtains back up.

We knew a few days before that Hitler had shot himself in his bunker. So the war would be over soon. When it was announced that the war was over, everyone went crazy and, as the song says, the lights went on all over the world.

* *

IT WAS SUNNY on that Tuesday morning, May 8, 1945. It wasn't even raining. The church bells began to ring everywhere. Even on our street we were kissing and hugging people we didn't even know, and crying and laughing at the same time.

That evening our wonderful Prime Minister, Winston Churchill, or Winny as everyone called him, spoke on the wireless in his growling bulldog voice, and told the whole of Britain that the war was over after five long hard years. Of course the Japanese were still at it, he said, but they too would soon be beaten.

"Mum," I said, "I'm going to the club to see who's around."

"Be careful, Kitty," she said.

And I ran to the club.

Some of the boys were there and so were Esther Levy and Hetty Schaffer, happy and excited like me.

"Let's go up West," someone said, and so we went.

The buses must have stopped because we walked through the city, past St. Paul's, all of us singing and laughing until we came to The Strand. People were throwing down paper streamers from windows. Others were wearing funny paper hats, and everyone was everyone's friend, kissing and hugging all the way.

When we came to The Strand the boys saw a wheelbarrow on the pavement, the kind that the builders use to haul bricks and concrete. It had enormous wheels and a big long handle. But it was empty.

Davie Marks said, "You girls get in the barrow and

we'll push you to Eros in Piccadilly."

What a lark that was. They pushed and we laughed, up the Haymarket to Leicester Square. And then, there was Eros, or rather a soldier and his girl standing and kissing where Eros, the God of Love, used to stand. Eros had been put in storage for the duration of the war, and the soldier and his girl were trying to take its place. Everyone was singing and dancing around them and cheering them on. Yanks from Rainbow Corner, just by Eros, were grabbing and kissing girls.

Hetty said, "Let's go to Buckingham Palace."

We left the barrow on the street for someone else to use and we loped and danced arm in arm to Pall Mall. Crowds and crowds were doing the same. Young people were climbing up lampposts, even clambouring onto the statue of Queen Victoria outside the Palace, and policemen didn't even try to stop them.

With darkness approaching, instead of searchlights scanning the sky, fireworks were shooting up from the parks nearby. Then a roar went up, and King George and Queen Elizabeth and the two princesses, Elizabeth and Margaret Rose, came out on the balcony of Buckingham Palace. The King, in his faulty stammer, thanked the people for their courage and God for saving the nation, and everyone sang *God Save the King*.

Then silence for a minute, and another roar went up: "We want Winny! We want Winny!" Prime Minister Winston Churchill came out on the balcony, a cigar in his hand, waving to the crowd, a great big smile on his chubby face. In his gravelly voice, he thanked the nation for helping him to lead the country to victory. But he said that there was still a lot to be done and that life would be hard for a while yet. But, he said, no more bombs and no more shelters. That was all that everyone wanted to hear. A great cheer went up and everyone began singing, *For He's a Jolly Good Fellow.*

We walked home, arms around each other through the same streets which I had walked with my Mum on the 10th of May, four years before. Some places were repaired but there were still a lot of bombed-out sites. They would be rebuilt one day, I knew.

When we got home, after midnight, neighbours were still standing on the street, watching the fireworks and talking about making a street party the next day. The bells were still ringing in the church at the end of our street and beer was being given to everyone from the local Truman's Brewery. My Dad, who never drank, helped himself, and even tried to give my Mum some. I couldn't believe it, she even took a sip, squeezing his arm, as if scared to let him go. Theresa was somewhere in the crowd, too, drinking and joking with the rest. Uncle Yudi, of course, didn't need any urging, and was drinking and singing the naughty music-hall songs that he used to teach me, and he too was kissing all the women on the street.

Soon life would go back to normal. But I heard someone say, "Do you remember what normal was?"

I'm not sure I really did.

Acknowledgments

THIS STORY saw the light of day in a long series of George Brown College's Writing for Children workshops led by my first enthusiast, Peter Carver, and held in the inspirational book-lined upper chamber of Mabel's Fables Children's Bookstore on Mount Pleasant Road in Toronto. With the encouragement and feedback from Peter and my classmates who heard every word, I developed the story chapter by chapter, benefiting at each step from their gentle critiques.

Special thanks go to the late Suzanne Burger, a teacher of Grade Three girls at Eitz Chaim Schools in Toronto, who twice read the entire manuscript to her students as a way of teaching about the human side of World War Two. Encouraged by their enthusiastic response, Suzanne invited me to visit her class and answer the girls' many questions about the war. The students created their own illustrations and presented them to me on my visits.

So many people who have read my book since it was published have asked me: "Nu? So when are you going to finish the story?" It's all that feedback that encouraged me to make this second edition a reality. I thank each and every one of you for that. And I would like also to thank my husband Ralph and daughter Suzanne for encouraging me to complete this project, and my late son Phillip, whose response to the original manuscript was, "It's great, Mum. Go for it!"

Kitty (Simmonds) Wintrob
Toronto, July 2014

Other Fine Titles from Now and Then Books

❦ **A Basket of Apples: Stories by Shirley Faessler.** The author brings the magic of a born storyteller to these linked stories about a coteries of Jewish immigrants in Toronto's Kensington Market in the 1920s and 1930s. "Nothing short of a masterpiece."—*Jewish Daily Forward (2014)*

❦ **Only Yesterday: Collected Pieces on the Jews of Toronto,** by Benjamin Kayfetz and Stephen Speisman. Eighteen evocative pieces about Toronto's old downtown Jewish community—its people, synagogues, Yiddish theatres and newspapers, and former 'Ward' and Spadina neighbourhoods. Enhanced with 144 historic photographs and illustrations, many taken by Speisman.

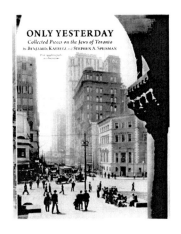

9 780991 900930